MW01120480

The Vulnerability of Corporate Reputation

DOI: 10.1057/9781137547378.0001

Other Palgrave Pivot titles

Simon Massey and Rino Coluccello: **Eurafrican Migration: Legal, Economic and Social Responses to Irregular Migration**

Duncan McDuie-Ra: **Debating Race in Contemporary India**

Andrea Greenbaum: **The Tropes of War: Visual Hyperbole and Spectacular Culture**

Kristoffer Kropp: **A Historical Account of Danish Sociology: A Troubled Sociology**

Monika E. Reuter: **Creativity – A Sociological Approach**

M. Saiful Islam: **Pursuing Alternative Development: Indigenous People, Ethnic Organization and Agency**

Justin DePlato: **American Presidential Power and the War on Terror: Does the Constitution Matter?**

Christopher Perkins: **The United Red Army on Screen: Cinema, Aesthetics and the Politics of Memory**

Susanne Lundin: **Organs for Sale: An Ethnographic Examination of the International Organ Trade**

Margot Finn and Kate Smith: **New Paths to Public Histories**

Gordon Ade-Ojo and Vicky Duckworth: **Adult Literacy Policy and Practice: From Intrinsic Values to Instrumentalism**

Brendan Howe: **Democratic Governance in Northeast Asia: A Human-Centred Approach to Evaluating Democracy**

Evie Kendal: **Equal Opportunity and the Case for State Sponsored Ectogenesis**

Joseph Watras: **Philosophies of Environmental Education and Democracy: Harris, Dewey, and Bateson on Human Freedoms in Nature**

Christos Kourtelis: **The Political Economy of Euro-Mediterranean Relations: European Neighbourhood Policy in North Africa**

Liz Montegary and Melissa Autumn White (editors): **Mobile Desires: The Politics and Erotics of Mobility Justice**

Anna Larsson and Sanja Magdalenić: **Sociology in Sweden: A History**

Philip Whitehead: **Reconceptualising the Moral Economy of Criminal Justice: A New Perspective**

Robert Kerr: **How Postmodernism Explains Football and Football Explains Postmodernism: The Billy Clyde Conundrum**

Ilan Bijaoui: **The Open Incubator Model: Entrepreneurship, Open Innovation, and Economic Development in the Periphery**

DOI: 10.1057/9781137547378.0001

palgrave▸pivot

The Vulnerability of Corporate Reputation: Leadership for Sustainable Long-Term Value

Peter Verhezen

MBS – University of Melbourne, Australia
University of Antwerp, Belgium

IFC – World Bank Group, Asia Pacific,
Verhezen & Associates Ltd,
Singapore-Indonesia

palgrave
macmillan

DOI: 10.1057/9781137547378.0001

First published 2015 by
PALGRAVE MACMILLAN

Palgrave Macmillan in the UK is an imprint of Macmillan Publishers Limited, registered in England, company number 785998, of Houndmills, Basingstoke, Hampshire RG21 6XS.

Palgrave Macmillan in the US is a division of St Martin's Press LLC, 175 Fifth Avenue, New York, NY 10010.

Palgrave Macmillan is the global academic imprint of the above companies and has companies and representatives throughout the world.

Palgrave® and Macmillan® are registered trademarks in the United States, the United Kingdom, Europe and other countries.

ISBN: 978–1–137–54736–1 EPUB
ISBN: 978–1–137–54737–8 PDF
ISBN: 978–1–137–54735–4 Hardback

A catalogue record for this book is available from the British Library.

A catalog record for this book is available from the Library of Congress.

www.palgrave.com/pivot

DOI: 10.1057/9781137547378

To our late parents, Annie-Charlotte Dekeyser and Jozef Verhezen,

▶ *who taught us the importance of the Golden Rule through emphasizing love, light and justice,*

generating kindness and trustworthiness,

which subsequently almost always resulted in a "good name" or reputation

DOI: 10.1057/9781137547378.0001

> *This was the Golden Age that, without coercion, without laws, spontaneously nurtured the good and the true. There was no fear or punishment: there were no threatening words to be read, fixed in bronze, no crowd of supplicants fearing the judge's face: they lived safely without protection.*
>
> Ovid, *The Metamorphoses*

> *The heart has its reasons, which reason does not know*
>
> Blaise Pascal, *Pensées*

DOI: 10.1057/9781137547378.0001

Contents

palgrave▶**pivot**

www.palgrave.com/pivot

Introductory Remarks: The Traps of Maximizing Shareholder Value

Abstract: *Bad corporate behavior potentially blackens the corporate reputation of the firm, undermining the relationships and trust on which an organization is established. Trust is the glue that holds any group or organization together. Pursuing opportunistic profit maximization at any cost seems to be counterproductive if considered over a longer time period. A more nuanced framework may be more compelling and sensible, in which organizations embrace the goals of serving their customers and respecting their employees and society at large.*

Verhezen, Peter. *The Vulnerability of Corporate Reputation: Leadership for Sustainable Long-Term Value.* Basingstoke: Palgrave Macmillan, 2015. DOI: 10.1057/9781137547378.0002.

This book is about how reputation should be acknowledged by boards to promote and establish good governance within existing legal and regulatory contexts that allows organizations to create more "sustainable" and meaningful results. This is a chapter about board members who become guardians, stewards and custodians of the organization, whose reputation and foresight could benefit the organization they are mandated to steer, to lead and to control.

The reputation of the leadership of many multinational companies has been tainted because of mismanagement during the recent global financial crisis. After the dramatic collapse of the banking sector in 2008–2009, there ensued a massive erosion of trust across industries. Bankers in particular and the corporate elite in general across the Western Hemisphere were seen to have little regard for their own stakeholders or the wider public interest. Hardly 43 percent of people in the West – though slightly higher in developing countries – trust CEOs of large organization,[1] largely because of questionable business practices like conflicts of interest, dishonest or corrupt behavior, environmental dumping and extremely high executive compensations.

When executives apparently do not need to bear possible losses for their mistakes, it hardly encourages good decision making.[2] Asymmetrical incentives allow bankers to "gamble with investors' money."[3] Bankers disproportionately benefited from bonuses but were insulated from the negative consequences of risks. Without having *skin in the game,* business will create bad decision making. A thriving economy needs risk-taking innovative entrepreneurs. Risk as such is unproblematic for society when those entrepreneurs or executives or board members who make decisions also bear the consequences of those decisions. The current explicit and especially implicit guarantees by government to bail out banks to prevent a complete economic meltdown unambiguously creates moral hazards[4] and may aggravate the (systemic) risks.[5] Were those bankers motivated by shortsighted greed or pushed by distorted incentive systems and relentless peer pressure?

I like to explicitly thank my friend and mentor Howard Dick (Professorial Fellow at the University of Melbourne) who critically commented on the early versions of a number of chapters, and my friend Yvo Vandeweyer for critically reading Chapter 2. I also like to express my gratitude to my sister Klara Verhezen and her partner Piet Taghon for continuously being there for me when necessary, to my uncle Charles Verhezen s.j. who continues to watch over me, and, of course, to my partner Linda Viyantimala Takko for her unwavering support and love.

It takes years for organizations to build a good reputation. Yet bad news or a crisis can destroy it in a manner of seconds. Being in the headlines for all the wrong reasons, the erosion of customer or investor trust can be sudden and dramatic. Corporate leaders as good stewards for shareholders and other stakeholders are therefore expected to guard assets from reputational loss. **Trust**[6] is the glue that holds any group or organization together and binds it with a coalition of key stakeholders. Reputation and its accounting representation as "goodwill" may be seen as the aggregation of trust, but it always remains at risk. By analogy, reputation may be seen as something like coastal sand dunes, a protective barrier built up over time but always at risk of rapid erosion by storms and tides. To extend the analogy, the ocean is public opinion.

Losing the battle for public perception can have dire consequences. Revealed bad corporate behavior potentially blackens the *corporate reputation* of the firm, undermining the relationships and trust on which an organization is established. Nike's corporate reputation, for instance, took a full decade to recover from the 1993 customer boycott over sweatshop allegations in Asia. BP's Deepwater Horizon debacle in 2010 has had dramatic effect on its share price and resulted in a significant leadership reshuffle. And banks in Europe and the United States have lost so much trust that they hardly can fill outstanding Information and Communications Technology (ICT) jobs since new IT graduates prefer to work at more cool places than banks.

Short-term profit maximization almost inevitably makes organizations more vulnerable to sudden loss of reputation, because the interests of managers and shareholders are privileged over employees, customers and society at large. These matters should all be addressed by a sound strategy that positions an organization in a dynamic and changing environment over a more than ten-year time horizon. Five years has now become a fairly standard period of tenure for a CEO. Moreover, pressure of the day-to-day expectations of financial markets, combined with the lure of performance pay for senior executives that is linked to the share price, have generated an epidemic of myopia. In consequence, employees work on the knife-edge of dismissal through cost cutting, customers are exploited and the public at large is treated with misleading and disdainful public relations.

Yet at the same time there has been a countervailing expectation, with some sanctions, for greater social accountability. CEOs now have to give attention to the usual economic costs and to the often hidden social and

DOI: 10.1057/9781137547378.0002

environmental costs that operations may generate. Organizations do not live in a social vacuum and, therefore, decisions at corporations are not just dealing with economic choices but likely will have social consequences. Hence why reputation management has become so crucial? Organizations that succeed today in this increasingly open environment are those whose operations are founded on the premise of a clearly expressed purpose supported by a set of values that have been engrained in the DNA of the organization. Such purpose internally enlightens and inspires the organization and is reflected in its enhanced reputation among shareholders and stakeholders alike. A well-regarded and reputable organization is admired for its brand identity as well as for what it stands for in terms of values and concern for its broader environment. In other words, the organization may constitute an integral part of the community and behaves accordingly, being respected by its employees, customers, suppliers and investors.

Enlightened managers are therefore now torn between the relentless expectation of financial markets for ever-increasing shareholder value and the relentless scrutiny of globally networked media for socially responsible behavior. Somehow a compromise must be struck. The path of least resistance, most commonly followed, is to respond to the most pressing stakeholders, namely, shareholders, while seeking to soothe and placate other external stakeholders through slick public relations and a façade of "corporate social responsibility." This approach can work quite well for a time but it increases reputational risk and therefore may not be a viable long-term strategy. If something goes badly wrong, if public expectations are no longer met and behavior is exposed to the glare of public scrutiny, the organization may not only suffer serious damage to its brand but even cease to be believed at all. This may be corporate Ground Zero. When such a crisis strikes, an organization has several ways to react.

Externally, policymakers may react to crises by setting up stricter *rules and oversight mechanisms* that attempt to impose upon corporate leaders what to do and how to comply with these rules. A second reaction is to internally set up an *incentive system* that encourages risk-taking performance within legal boundaries and that financially rewards executives for higher returns on investment.[7] Unfortunately, corporate executives increasingly resemble "corporate robots" serving powerful organizations and institutes, depriving employees and customers from any sensible purpose. No doubt better rules and smarter incentives can play an

DOI: 10.1057/9781137547378.0002

important role in improving the way organizations perform. But externally imposed rules and internally organized incentive systems, sticks and carrots, will never fully capture the potential energy that resides within an organizations. Neither rules (no matter how detailed, well implemented and properly monitored), nor (pecuniary) incentives (no matter how clever) will be enough to resolve the underlying causes of distrust of organizations we currently face. Relying on ineffective rules and distorted incentive mechanisms only would be a mistake. We need more than strict rules and stringent oversight or just adapt the corporate incentive systems.

Believing that the implementation of mere pecuniary incentives will result in desired organizational outcomes is naive at best. Even worse, (over)regulation and misguided rules can kill skills and create red tape, whereas misaligned incentives can kill the desire to achieve "good" profits.[8] The current accounting principles and financial metrics[9] gauging for financial success focus mainly on quarterly/annual profitability regardless of whether those profits represent rewards from building long-term relationships or the spoils from abusing them. Taking exuberant or badly misunderstood risks and cutting corners where possible seem to be tolerated as long as the firm generates "profits" for its shareholders and associated partners. Narrowly focusing on this kind of "bad" profit at any cost[10] seems to be the overall measure of successful management, rewarded at and by *Wall Street* and other major stock exchanges.[11] It seems to encourage "a governance system for crooks."[12] Moreover, competitive pressure push banks to engage in the same activities to "keep up with the Goldmans." Citigroup CEO Chuck Prince put it famously in 2007 just before the crisis erupted: "as long as the music is playing, you've got to get up and dance." But while Citi and other financial institutions at Wall Street were dancing, their leadership did not give enough attention to the risks involved. Nonetheless, their leaders got away with it: Prince's reported USD 68 million legally condoned departure package after losing more than half of Citi's stock value was not exactly justifiable from a socioethical perspective.

Maybe it is time to transform the prevailing drive to focus on short-term profitability into a broader more holistic or systemic socioeconomic framework. Investors' myopia is less related to their eagerness for quarterly profitability than to their unwillingness to embrace socioenvironmental objectives that may (or may not) strengthen long-term corporate value. Stock prices primarily reflect the current value of the

DOI: 10.1057/9781137547378.0002

company's net assets and its earnings' growth potential. However, key stakeholders' concerns are not directly valued in this stock price mechanism. One alternative to broaden this evaluation is to govern and manage corporate reputation by ensuring the ability to assume external actors' perspectives and by engraining some of these different viewpoints into new strategies that provides real solutions to some of the stakeholders' challenges and concerns.

Our argument boils down to the proposition that in this increasingly open and transparent world, organizations and their leaders will need to adhere to *best corporate governance principles* and take *wise decisions* to constitute and maintain the trust of its critical stakeholders. In other words, when decisions are pursued whose aim is to clearly fulfill a sensible and aspiring purpose of the organization without harming anybody or anything else, trust will be regained. And such trust between direct involved stakeholders will also enhance the *reputation* of the organizations in the eyes of people who may not have experienced direct contact with the organization. It is pressure to sustain this corporate reputation in the eyes of critical stakeholders that will partially enable the organization to initiate a virtuous circle of appropriate behavior, allowing the providers of capital and a number of stakeholders to benefit from the company. Businesses build informal networks or relationships with relevant and critical stakeholders that help secure trust, commitment and loyalty in the absence of effective legal enforcement. And even when there is well-functioning legal and regulatory framework, good relationships or social capital constitute the basis for achieving good reputation. When the organization has learnt to embrace unavoidable tensions between different stakeholders and subtly handle ambiguous paradoxes, it may achieve "greatness" and thus corporate *reputational excellence*.

Despite a deep interest in the ethical behavior in organizations, this will not be another book on battering the walls of greedy corporate elite, nor does it explicitly focus on the importance of a revised and more "enlightened" capitalism. Instead this book is about how reputation should be acknowledged by boards to promote and establish good governance within existing legal and regulatory contexts that allows organizations to create more "sustainable" and meaningful results. This is a book about board members who become guardians, stewards and custodians of the organization, whose reputation and foresight could benefit the organization they are mandated to steer and to lead. It is about board members whose managerial wisdom makes organizations

DOI: 10.1057/9781137547378.0002

excel through best corporate governance practices that go beyond mere compliance to rules and regulations, reduce potential reputation risks and gain reputational excellence with a more balanced use of both intrinsic and extrinsic motivators. It is about signaling the corporate purpose and intentions to its primary stakeholders, whereby the "shadow of the future" plays an important role in building up a good reputation. It is about relationship building between the firms and loyal customers and suppliers and committed employees.

Guided by a clear and enlightened soulful purpose and mission – and their underlying (ethical humane) values and vision – leaders can always improve their decision making. PepsiCo's vision of "performance with a purpose" under the leadership of Ms. Nooyi acknowledges the importance of corporate social responsibility and stakeholder strategy. The question is whether this aspirational rhetoric of PepsiCo will convince Wall Street investors alike. Similarly, the CEO of Unilever, Paul Polman, insists on the importance of environmentally sustainable products to achieve profitability. However, without change in customers' behavior, Unilever will not be able to dramatically reduce its own ecological footprint and ultimately may fail to achieve its "Sustainable Life Plan." How to address such paradoxical conundrum of reputational excellence? Pragmatic practitioners like Ms. Nooyi and Mr. Polman are motivated to fulfill that purpose as good as possible. Obviously, financial performance remains a necessity to survive, but also in need for sensible infusion from broader defined objectives. Maximizing only profitability may become a misleading and slippery slope over a longer period, and even undermine its initial reputation of being a good financial performer.

It is the board's obligation to monitor, control and steer the firm's executives to exercise the right choices. One of the major fiduciary duties of a board requires them to oversee the protection of the firm's assets, tangible as well as intangible. Wise leadership and boards are able to perceive the contextual situation, have the appropriate intuitive feelings or sense about it, assess and deliberate about what is appropriate in these circumstances and are able to act accordingly. In other words, corporate governance is the institutionalized foundation for improved decision making that is correlated with corporate reputation. Well-functioning boards definitely create trust. Warren Buffett, founder and chairman of Berkshire, the "oracle of Ohama," has consistently made "wise" investment decisions, resulting in a stellar personal and corporate reputation that lead to an incredible stock price of over USD 200,000 per share on

August 18, 2014! Despite this incredible consistent increase of the stock price over those decades – and without degrading Warren Buffet's proven business acumen – one could question whether the market evaluation of stock is the only criterion to judge someone's performance in an organization.

As the world continues to get smaller through the advancement of information and communication technology, the mutual interdependence of organizations and their stakeholders grows larger by the day. The increasingly interdependent and connected world creates *changed expectations* that affect the overall demand and require a higher level of corporate and individual accountability. And as the world continues to get smaller, the **mutual interdependence** of the organization and their stakeholders grows larger. To optimize its performance, organizations rely increasingly upon the effective utilization of not only their own resources, but also of those of others. To achieve coordinated cooperation that relies on other organizations' resources, one needs to create trustworthy relationships. Therefore, the key to success and development is gaining trust of present and potential stakeholders. Earning the trust of the different stakeholders is key to mobilizing resources towards a common vision or purpose. Having superb relationships with most of your relevant stakeholders will definitely help to enhance the corporate reputation, consequently be better prepared to waver potential crises. The firm can draw upon this [symbolic] capital of reputation in times of crisis. In that sense, *reputation functions as an insurance policy* upon which it can fall back in case a crisis erupts.

We argue that a slightly broader interpretation of the mainstream shareholder value theory will equip a board better to proactively and occasionally reactively deal with reputational crises. To stay in the game, organizations rely increasingly upon collaborative efforts and joint forces. In order to be able to access these resources of others, organizations need to create trustworthy relationships. Indeed, in a digitized business context where clusters of collaboration reinforce each other's competitive strengths, individual and corporate reputation will function as the indicative beacon of trustworthiness and confidence. For instance, recently some big fashion names such as LVMH are using the familiarity of social media to make shopping easier on mobile devices worldwide; more than one third of online shopping is expected to take place on tablets and smartphones in the coming years[13] In developing African and emerging Asian countries, the use of smart phones for internet banking and e-payments will likely dramatically

DOI: 10.1057/9781137547378.0002

reshape the current banking competition. Reputation and trust here all play a crucial role in convincing potential customers and suppliers.

In order to safeguard corporate reputation, we believe that a board's responsibilities need to be interpreted in a broader and more integral perspective. This book is structured under two main headings: *reputation risk* on the downside of the probability/impact curve and *reputation excellence* on the upside of that curve. Although each of the four chapters and concluding remarks can be read independently as separated though interlinked pieces, this volume explores the common theme of the **significance of reputation and trust in business.**

Part I specifically focuses on the traditional topic of *reputation risk management*, that is, communication and crisis management. More specifically, Chapter 1 analyzes *outrage* and *fear* as possible causes of distrust and reputational damage. It attempts to indicate how to fine-tune traditional reputation measurements. By distinguishing "good" from "bad" profits, organizations institutionalize incentive systems and processes that help to reduce this mistrust. Chapter 2 focuses on the process of reputation that is essentially based on the distinction made in evolutionary and game theory between *direct* and *indirect reciprocity.*[14] The trustworthiness of the other party will be highly valued in "direct" exchanges, whereas corporate reputation fulfills a similar role in more "indirect" exchanges, especially when the information is quite asymmetric or not readily available. Paradoxically, gossiping about organizations and their leaders may enhance the mechanisms of beneficial reciprocal relationships and cooperation.

In Part II we shift our focus to *reputational excellence*. Chapter 3 asserts that within a digitized and interconnected sociobusiness context where transparency supposedly reigns, no organization seems to be able to escape stakeholders' scrutiny anymore. Information asymmetries will continue to exist in certain contexts. However, *acting responsibly, always*, seems to be the first step to prepare for reputation excellence. Taking stakeholders more seriously, both their ecological and social concerns, and engaging in more fulfilling relationships with those stakeholders will undoubtedly have a positive impact on the firm's reputation. That partially explains the growing importance of Corporate Social Responsibility (CSR) and Environmental, Social and Governance (ESG) in multinational organizations in securing a good corporate reputation. Subsequently, Chapter 4 describes how *boards* can embrace *"wise" decision making* that will enhance the chances of reputation excellence,

DOI: 10.1057/9781137547378.0002

which is an intangible but very valuable expression, having created good relationships with its critical stakeholders.

The concluding remarks emphasize how reputation, transcending the shadow of its own profile, could be a useful guideline for boards and top executives to help setting strategies and policies. However, seeking corporate reputation excellence is hindered by a number of current barriers. Four main recommendations are suggested to overcome those constraints: (1) a visionary purpose; (2) embracing collaborative innovation; (3) caring for "people, planet and profit" in this digitized world; and (4) acting wisely beyond compliance that could help to enrich its share- and stakeholders while minimizing ecological and social harm. Adhering to a different more holistic mindset will enable leadership to lift their organization to a higher level. Organizations will always remain dependent on others who may bestow upon it the label of "having a good corporate reputation." That is why corporate reputation remains **vulnerable**, which paradoxically could also constitute its strength.

As in most cases, our own upbringing and experiences colors our perspective. This book is no exception. Any perspective remains partial. We only can attempt to be as accurate and sincere as possible. Obviously, this book was only possible by standing on the shoulders of so many scholars, practitioners and wise people, too many to personally name but often referred to in the numerous footnotes. It goes without saying that any remaining weakness in argumentation remains my sole responsibility.

Notes

1   See http://www.edelman.com/2015-edelman-trust-barometer/. "Marked by declines in trust in the once impenetrable technology industry, trust levels in business decreased in 16 of 27 countries. The majority of countries now sit below 50 per-cent with regard to trust in business. Leading the declines were Canada, Argentina, Germany, Australia and Singapore, which all witnessed double-digits declines in trust in 2015 (−15, −12, −12, −11, and −10 points, respectively)."

2   We like to refer to the following interesting scholarly work by Roubini (2011); Shiller (2012); Rajan (2011); Admati and Hellwig (2013) that reveal the processes, causes and roots behind the global financial crisis of 2008–2009. Every entrepreneur knows that taking risks may bear some decent return worth the efforts taken. Bankers, however, do not seem to bear any downside

DOI: 10.1057/9781137547378.0002

risk for their bets on risky investments with other people's money. For an excellent overview of performance-based pay and how to hide risks behind profits in international banking, I highly recommend Admati and Hellwig's *The Bankers' New Clothes*.

3   See Admati and Hellwig (2013) and Zingales in "Committee Holds Hearing on the Causes and Effects of the Lehman Brothers Bankruptcy" in 2008. It seems that exuberant large rewards and a sense that "everyone is doing it" have eroded behavior codes focusing on clients' trust in international banking. Professor Luis Zingales, a colleague of Professor Admati at Chicago, believes that the Lehman Brothers' use of aggressive leverage (as many other Wall Street investment banks), emphasis on short-term debt financing, bad industry regulation, lack of transparency and market complacency due to the several years of juicy earnings were the root causes. He also indicated that mortgage derivatives were evaluated on historical grounds, and firms had subsequently failed to factor in an ahistorical decline in lending standards and fall in real estate prices. Although it was evident that greed was a contributing factor, there were many more complicated and equally important causative factors. Billions or trillions of dollars in shareholder value were destroyed during the GFC.

4   In **economics**, moral hazard occurs when one person takes more **risks** because someone else bears the burden of those risks. A moral hazard may occur where the actions of one party may change to the detriment of another after a **financial transaction** has taken place. Moral hazard occurs under a type of **information asymmetry** where the risk-taking party to a transaction knows more about its intentions than the party paying the consequences of the risk. More broadly, moral hazard occurs when the party with more information about its actions or intentions has a tendency or incentive to behave inappropriately from the perspective of the party with less information. Moral hazard also arises in a **principal-agent problem**, where one party, called an agent, acts on behalf of another party, called the principal. The agent usually has more information about his or her actions or intentions than the principal does, because the principal usually cannot completely monitor the agent. The agent may have an incentive to act inappropriately (from the viewpoint of the principal) if the interests of the agent and the principal are not aligned.

5   In other words, as long as their "skin is in the game," and as long as they do not harm others who have little control over these decisions, there is no problem that risks are generously rewarded. As Admati and Hellwig convincingly argue (2013), bankers do not bear the full consequences of their decisions, and they can seriously harm others who will have little control over them, as the financial mortgage crisis of 2007–2009 and the subsequent aftermath economic downturn have proven.

DOI: 10.1057/9781137547378.0002

6   Govier (1998). Trust is in essence an attitude of positive expectation about other people, a sense that they are basically well intentioned and unlikely to harm us. To trust people is to expect that they will act well and that they will take our interests into account and not harm us. A trustworthy person can be defined as someone who has both good intentions and reasonable competence. Trust is a relational attitude: one person trusts another, or several others, or a group.

7   Pink (2009). Under certain circumstances, especially when dealing with creative more heuristic-oriented right brain challenges, financial rewards and goal setting can undermine the effectiveness of the tool. Narrow goal setting like quarterly results – which restricts our view from broader dimensions – can even induce unethical behavior. Although goal setting can increase effectiveness by concentrating on the mind, such narrowed focus comes with a cost, that is, crowding out ethical behavior. Pink describes Motivation 1.0 as mere survival, whereas Motivation 2.0 has been derived from 19th-century efficiency thinking where rewards and punishments were used to incite better output for routine jobs. However, over the past couple of decades, our knowledge-based economy demands a more *heuristic creative approach* – rather than an *algorithm for complex routine jobs*. Motivation 3.0 can be described as a situation in which people find intrinsic meaning in those creative solution-seeking challenges that cannot be induced by mere pecuniary motivators. Under Motivation 2.0 one could reward for more output of the same and punishment for less output. Under fundamentally different circumstances, that "carrot and stick" approach may not work that effectively, since a meaningful purpose, autonomy and mastery are now the main motivating drivers of job satisfaction.

8   We borrow this concept distinction from Fred Reichheld's interesting book *The Ultimate Question. How Net Promotor Companies Can Thrive in a Customer-Driven World* (2011). I am grateful to Warren Weeks, CEO of Cubit Media Research, who introduced me to the book.

9   Lazonick (2014). He argues that the current accounting principles are undermining sincere wealth creation or prosperity for shareholders and other relevant stakeholders. Indeed, currently, corporate profitability is not translating into economic prosperity in the United States. Instead of investing profits in innovation and productive capabilities, top management and executives are spending them on gigantic stock repurchases. These buybacks may increase stock prices in the short term and thus "indirectly" the bonuses, but in the long term they undermine income equality, job stability and growth. The buybacks mostly serve the interests of executives, much of whose compensation is in the form of stock. Lazonick argues that corporations should be banned from repurchasing their shares on the open market. Executives' excessive stock-based pay should be reined in. Workers

and taxpayers should be represented on corporate boards according to Laloux (2014) for example, quite a drastic suggestion, though German boards do already have mandatory employee representatives on their boards. And governments should reform the tax system so that it rewards value creation, not value extraction.

10   Imagine a company that pollutes a river and does not pay for the damage that the pollution imposes on people and firms downstream. That company may be a world leader in its markets, but its products are (relatively) cheap(er than the competition) because the costs of its pollution are borne by others and, therefore, its apparent success is not beneficial to society at all. Or imagine a company that misleads its customers or deliberately evades due taxes; such successful profitable firms are not necessarily benefiting society at large.

11   Admittedly, the socioeconomic context on Continental Europe and their bourses is slightly different from the Anglo-Saxon New York-London axis. The latter emphasizes individual property rights and the maximizing of profits of those private assets, whereas the former has built in more socioeconomic constraints in terms of welfare state interventionism. The question is whether there is a converging trend occurring, especially now that overseas stock exchanges are being merged, which may have an effect on long-term rules and regulations.

12   This notion of "governance for crooks" is borrowed from Osterlom and Frey (2004).

13   *Financial Times*, August 18, 2014.

14   We base the distinction on the breakthrough analysis of Martin Nowak, whose Evolutionary Dynamics has confirmed the importance of "altruistic reciprocity" in most exchanges, including long-term business relationships.

DOI: 10.1057/9781137547378.0002

Part I
The Complexity of Governing Reputational Risks

Verhezen, Peter. *The Vulnerability of Corporate Reputation: Leadership for Sustainable Long-Term Value.* Basingstoke: Palgrave Macmillan, 2015. DOI: 10.1057/9781137547378.0003.

▶

DOI: 10.1057/9781137547378.0003

Concerns among boards about their reputation and the risks to reputation have increased dramatically in the past decade. Globally, *reputation risk* has become one of the top risk concerns of any CEO or board, next to *retaining managerial talent* and *sustaining creative innovation*. Owing to the amorphous and ambiguous nature of reputation, senior executives and board members find this "risk of risks"[1] harder to manage compared to any other risk. Not only is it difficult to measure reputation risk, but hardly 60 percent of most (global) companies have prepared a plan in place to manage reputation risk.[2] Responsibilities to manage and reduce reputational risks are often fragmented and therefore poorly coordinated, which in itself can increase the reputation risk. Obviously, reputation risk will not fade away by itself.

Never has trust in business been lower, yet never has it been more important in business exchanges and building relationships. CEOs are among the least trusted professions, just barely ahead of used-car dealers and politicians.[3] Business has been profoundly affected by a decline in trust following the wake of corporate scandals and a turbulent economy, by the disillusionment over excessive executive pay despite the crisis.

Digitized social media have empowered a wide range of stakeholders. It goes without saying that the globalization of companies and the digitization of information and knowledge have greatly contributed to a continuous scrutiny of corporate motivations and corporate behavior. The amalgam of different opinions and expectations and beliefs and values constitute corporate reputation. Bad fate can suddenly strike. However, irresponsible corporate behavior may be less forgivable, possibly causing a corporate reputational crisis. How to govern those possible or immanent reputational risks? The first part of the book will attempt to address how to reduce the causes of reputation risks to potentially increase the trustworthiness, reliability and credibility of a firm.

Notes

1 Tonello 2007.
2 See the FERMA Survey 2012; Schreiber 2011.
3 Gallup News 2008; Edelman Trust Barometer 2014–2015.

DOI: 10.1057/9781137547378.0003

1
Winning the "Hearts and Minds" of Stakeholders

Abstract: *Managing corporate reputation requires boards and top management to assume different perspectives, and to focus on a number of objectives that are well beyond mere profit maximization. Internal drivers of values, beliefs, purpose and organizational culture are an effective counterforce to behavior that only seeks short-term profitability at all costs. Reputation risk management aims at increasing the odds of good outcomes and reducing the odds of bad outcomes. Good reputation management relies not only on vigilance and staying informed, but also on a readiness to respond quickly and effectively to challenges or perceived problems as and when they arise.*

Verhezen, Peter. *The Vulnerability of Corporate Reputation: Leadership for Sustainable Long-Term Value.* Basingstoke: Palgrave Macmillan, 2015. DOI: 10.1057/9781137547378.0004.

DOI: 10.1057/9781137547378.0004

Over the past decade, most corporations have undergone a change from providing products and services to a focus of selling experiences or a solution. Starbucks does not merely sell coffee; it sells an experience. Xerox does not just sell photocopy machines; it leases them out because it provides solutions to universities, design companies and publishers. Both rely heavily on building and maintaining relationships with their primary customers. Such relationships are based on trust. Cognitive and affective trust in organizations is gained over a period of time potentially resulting in a good reputation. A firm's reputation consists of what others are publicly saying about the firm. The more business models are being built on experiences and solutions, the higher the stakes have become. If you live by the brand and its reputation, you also can die by the brand.[1]

1.1   Potential causes of reputational risks

Managing corporate reputation requires boards and top management to assume different perspectives, and to focus on a number of objectives that are well beyond mere profit maximization. Obviously, those different perspectives occasionally clash or demand a certain trade-off. Nonetheless, developing "good corporate reputation" will need "wise" leadership, supported by appropriate processes, procedures and capabilities and aligned with an integrated strategic perspective. Concretely, management and boards need to maintain or strengthen the relationships of trust in the company.

Corporate scandals like Exxon's Valdez oil spill incident in Alaska in 1989 or the BP's Deepwater Horizon oil leak in 2010, to name just two out of a long list, are reputation killers for these companies and for their managers and board members. The opposite is also true. The Tylenol crisis in 1982 at Johnson & Johnson, for instance, has been an example where the company has developed an inspiring reputational narrative underwriting the values and belief system of the company, as mandated in its *Credo*. The consequence is a stellar corporate reputation groomed over the years, despite some hick-ups lately. These examples indicate that enhancing trust is among the most important tasks for management, especially in times of crises. Kellogg's professor Daniel Diermeier developed a "trust radar" to analyze reputational risks. He focuses on four crucial factors in building trust in organizations – *transparency*, *expertise*, *commitment* and *empathy* – during or before a crisis.[2] By narrowing

DOI: 10.1057/9781137547378.0004

management focus on expertise only, and largely ignoring empathy, leaders and their organizations usually aggravate the crisis situation. During moments of crisis we view corporations less as impersonal purveyors of goods and services and more as members of our community. And if those corporate citizens, members of the community, are perceived not to care about us, they look out of touch or even "monstrous" to us.

Nonetheless, reputation means different things to different people, but it should be clear that reputational risks extend beyond the legal boundaries of the firm and are often related to *moral disgust* or *emotional fear*. Reputational crises are almost always about trust! The most difficult crises are those in which the organization believes that it does not bear any wrongdoing, but everyone else thinks it does. A crisis about trust always needs strong pragmatic leadership and a strategic and mindful sophisticated understanding to move beyond mere emotional reactions. And that will require leadership that replaces the management monologue approach with genuine dialogues, focusing on values and collaboration to regain or strengthen trust. Switching from a mere legalistic to a trust-based approach will definitely help. A trustworthy leadership will need to embrace cognitive, emotional as well as moral dimensions in dealing with a reputational crisis. It will need to balance analytical expert reasoning with intuitive and empathetic feelings for its concerned stakeholders, occasionally willing to take bold but intelligent risks to address a reputational crisis.

1.2   What is corporate reputation?

Reputation is a reflection of how well or how badly different groups of interested people – stakeholders – view an organization or perceive an individual. Reputation consists of perceptions – whether "true" or "false" – held by others about that organization or individual. In this definition reputation is (1) based on perceptions that imply that it is somewhat out of control of the particular firm or individual and (2) is an aggregate perception of all stakeholders that highlights its social and collective character. Indeed, reputations are socially shared impressions that are based on "collectives."[3]

Others argue that corporate reputation refers to the "observers' collective judgments of a corporation based on assessments of the financial, social, and environmental impacts attributed to the corporation over time."[4] Corporate reputation can therefore be defined as "a relatively stable, issue specific aggregate perceptual representation of a company's past actions and future prospects compared against some standard,"[5] or compared with other leading rivals.[6]

Corporate reputation embraces both (1) a *cognitive* component as in the valuation of the company's attributes and (2) *affective* reactions of customers, investors, employees and the public at large. This combination of affective and cognitive components allows us to define reputation as an attitudinal construct, denoting subjective emotional and cognitive-based mindsets.[7] Despite some remaining disagreements among scholars because of the elusive and "intangible" nature of reputation, progress has been made in defining and understanding corporate reputation.

Reputation can be perceived as a judgment or actual perception of the firm by stakeholders or observers[8] and is a function of certain events exposing a corporate identity feature, be it a business practice, a behavioral incident or a characteristic of the products sold. Corporate reputation can be positive or negative; for example, stakeholders perceive the firm as being environmentally responsible, or stakeholders view the corporation as being harmful to the environment. *Reputation Capital* is obviously a valuable economic asset and can be defined as the perception of the firm by those stakeholders[9] whose relationship with the firm is directly instrumental to the pursuit of long-term growth and shareholder value.

A *(corporate) brand,* by contrast, tends to relate to what the corporation wants to be and how it tends to differentiate itself from competitors, rather than what it actually is.[10] Many scholars and practitioners alike have focused on developing tools to measure the intangible brand equity, but there is less clarity around what drives corporate reputation.

And despite the fact that many still use "identity," "image" and "reputation" interchangeably, a clear conceptual distinction should be made. "Identity" is the true essence of the corporation and its defining attributes are its mission, strategy, core ethical values, organizational culture and business practices. Identity is that which is most central, enduring and distinctive about an organization.[11] A *corporate identity* is primarily a function of the perception and knowledge of the organization by insiders.

"*Image,*" however, is how the corporation represents itself to the public. As such, *corporate image* is a function of mandatory disclosure, public relations, marketing (branding and advertising) efforts and other organizational initiatives that attempt to shape the impression people have of the firm. Organizational image is viewed as a desired image and therefore it can be described as an internal picture projected to an external audience. And an image can be manipulated.

One could argue that corporate identity refers to the collection of symbols that somehow refers to the underlying core or character of the firm whereas the corporate image can be defined as the impressions stakeholders have about the firm. The transition from identity to image is usually the result of smart public relations and marketing management that shapes the impression that people have of the firm. Image can possibly be shaped but not fully controlled by the management of the firm. Turning image into reputation will not succeed without some deliberate efforts.

Reputation, nonetheless, remains a relative or relational concept and depends on everything the organization does as an entity. Companies can and do have multiple reputations for different things with different people[12] as individuals usually have different identities.[13] It is rather difficult to have an aggregate measurement for reputation without suffering a loss in analytical rigor. For customers, value may be a fair price or quality. For employees, it may be a good job, good pay and good working conditions. For prospective talent, it may be a good place to work; for the community, it might be a company that is a good corporate citizen. For instance, Goldman Sachs[14] or JP Morgan may have a very strong reputation for being a top destination for finance MBAs, but it currently has a very poor reputation with international regulators or other noninvestment stakeholders.

Often, corporate reputation becomes the summation of a number of attributes and characteristics, as found in Fortune's Most Admired Companies, or Reputation Quotient ratings (by the Reputation Institute). Despite the variety of rudimentary techniques now available to quantify reputation risk – for instance, Reputation Quotient,[15] and RepTrak[16] – companies and investors still do not fully agree on a common set of metrics. Obviously, understanding how stakeholders think about the organization's attributes in terms of emotional appeal, products and services, financial performance, vision and leadership, workplace environment, governance and compliance and social responsibility may give a good indication about the corporate reputation. Strong corporate reputation helps to attract the best employee and managerial talents while it also fosters better employee retention. It may even lower or decrease average cost. That corporate reputation increases customers' confidence

DOI: 10.1057/9781137547378.0004

in products, resulting in price premiums and higher purchase rates and higher customer retention is well analyzed.[17] Moreover, companies showing a strong corporate reputation may also benefit from better access to capital markets and decreasing capital costs. Independently, empirical data have validated that firms with a favorable corporate reputation are more likely to maintain a higher profitability level over time.[18] No doubt that corporate reputation generates quite a number of benefits for the organization.

What frameworks or mindsets should be used to analyze corporate reputation? How to understand the main perspectives constituting corporate reputation?[19] Conceptually, three main frameworks are used to assess corporate reputation. The prevailing *Institutional Theory* emphasizes the context in which corporations build or lose corporate reputation, whereas the *Signaling Theory* uses the images and the impression of those images and identities to form, build and maintain a (corporate) reputation. Finally, a *Resource-Based Perspective* sees corporate reputation as a valuable asset in establishing a competitive advantage.

As we all know, trust can swiftly evaporate. It takes 20 years to build reputation and 5 minutes to ruin it. "We can afford to lose money – even a lot of money. But we cannot afford to lose reputation – even a shred of reputation. We must continue to measure every act against not only what is legal, but also what we would be happy to have written about on the front page of a national newspaper in an article written in an unfriendly but intelligent report," Warren Buffett reportedly said.[20] There can be no doubt that corporate reputation is in the spotlight and needs to be distinguished from media relations, image building or identity and status. Hence we here emphasize the risk component of reputation management. Corporations strive to minimize the chance that trust and credibility would be under attack or in jeopardy negatively affecting the financial bottom line of the organization. The **institutional context** in which corporate reputation can thrive will need to be treasured by corporate leadership. Good governance emphasizing risk minimization and the quest for reputation excellence are main factors to contribute to that goal. Indeed, excellence, backed up by appropriate corporate governance rules and mechanisms and sincere and reliable corporate communications often remain the optimal way to safeguard a good reputation over a longer period. Maintaining a good reputation or keeping reputation risks within reasonable limits has become more ambiguous and complex. A growing market transparency and an acceleration of scandal-prone

DOI: 10.1057/9781137547378.0004

search by the media – which is difficult to control – have contributed to this ambiguity. Institutional intermediaries, such as media and analysts, are considered as experts with superior access to organizational information. As a result, these institutional intermediaries may influence the opinions of the stakeholders of an organization.

Second, if we accept that organizations have multiple reputations – something for someone in a particular context – then we can argue that the value of that reputation lies in the *signal* that we want to send a stakeholder. In other words, when we are clear about which reputation, for what, and with whom it is being measured, we can act accordingly. Attempting to aggregate those different reputations may be unhelpful and it may reinforce the sense of an un-measurable notion. At the heart of reputation lies the direct experience of the different stakeholders, compared to their expectations. It is the observed or experienced behavior of the organizations and the individuals responsible and accountable within the organization that sits at the core of the organizational reputation. In other words, what we do matters, as past behavior and performance (partially) determine what we can expect from the organization in the future. Furthermore, a slightly more distant area of determining the reputation of an organization is based on what we have heard about the organization's activity: it remains a very indirect experience. Finally, there is the outer further circle of *gossip,* the mass of information that is not directly experienced but received secondhand. Since we are social animals, we often express opinions without any fact or supportive information or data behind them. Consequently, the main intermediaries affecting reputation – traditional media and social media outlets, analysts and investors, regulators, customers, employees – have become increasingly influential. Moreover, it seems that we manage organizations by trying to influence conscious processes and explicit knowledge.[21]

Finally, building reputation somehow implies that the organization or the individual builds "social capital" that encompasses the components of trust and credibility under specific societal, market and media conditions of the 21st century. Reputation is a key *corporate resource* that can be managed and accumulated. Building up a strong corporate reputation creates market barriers and can strengthen the company's strategic positioning in a competitive marketplace.[22] Corporate reputation can be exchanged for some legitimization of positions of power, social respect, a price premium for good and services offered, an increased willingness

DOI: 10.1057/9781137547378.0004

by others to hold equity stakes in times of crises, and an eagerness to invest preferably in the shares of the company.[23] The currency in all these exchange activities or "stakes"[24] is identical for all those involved, as expressed by trust. As an *intangible asset*, corporate reputation contributes to a firm's performance as it is affected by the assessment of the firm's stakeholders. Despite the fact that most agree that good corporate reputation clearly creates organizational value, it is much harder to quantify that value. A mathematical sure calculation of this intangible remains elusive.

Corporate reputation – understood as expectations about a firm's future behavior based on perceptions of past behavior or performance – is what stakeholders and people in general say about a company's character and performance. It is what the company stands for as perceived in their values. As such, a firm cannot simply build a reputation *per se*. The creation and building up of reputation is dependent on the successful execution of a number of activities that are nonetheless encapsulated in a strong financial performance.[25] Reputation is not an absolute; it remains a relative notion. Although reputation cannot be fully owned by organizations or an individual – since it consists of perceptions held by others based on direct experiences or what they hear indirectly – organizations, nonetheless, can exert certain control or influence over their reputation. Behaving well does not automatically guarantee a good reputation; organizations will need to communicate this good behavior effectively to the right stakeholders. Moreover, communication without the behavior to match what is being said will be perceived as "greenwashing" or mere public relations and will inflict greater damage on the organization's reputation than simply saying nothing.

1.2.1 Determinants of reputation risk

Risk is a reflection of inevitable uncertainty. It therefore refers to an event that can take place in an uncertain future. In this context, risk means being exposed to the possibility and impact of a bad (or good) outcome. Risk management aims to take deliberate actions to shift the odds favorably by *preventing* for certain events to occur or *preparing* for the impact in case the (negative) event takes place. *Prevention* strategies are meant to reduce the probability of a negative possible event to take place whereas *preparation* strategies are specifically designed to limit the negative impact of those threats or to embrace potential positive outcomes. Reputation risk management is about increasing the odds of good outcomes and reducing the odds of bad outcomes.

Reputation risk itself is determined mainly by three main factors.[26] First an *expectation-experience gap* can cause reputation risks. If one promotes a high-quality car at a premium price but within the first three years the car reports a number of mechanical failures, one can almost be sure that the reputation of the car brand will be tainted. Quite often, customer service is neglected in reputational management programs. By addressing particular challenges more systemically and attempting to find a solution to the source behind the lack of a good service, companies significantly reduce reputation risks, or even enhance their corporate reputation. Some years ago, when Singapore Airlines, quite unusual for them, left Changi Airport in Singapore for Frankfurt almost two hours late, the pilot apologized as in good custom. However, he added quite unexpectedly that he would try to make up for the lost time by speeding up a little in order to get the passengers in time to Frankfurt and allow them to get their connecting flights. Service is everything for Singapore Airlines and the cost to speed up has definitely been compensated by extreme loyal customers who believe in the outstanding reputation of Singapore Airlines as the best airline (or at least among the best) in the world, consistently and consciously serving their customers through coordinated efforts of the company's management. In this case, potential damage was turned to the firm's advantage creating a positive gap between experience and expectations.

Second, a *change in norms and beliefs*, behavior or policies, will affect firms. Nowadays, there is a clear trend in the market to produce more ecologically sound and eco-efficient products and services. The increased focus on corporate social responsible behavior is an expression of that trend. The "Ecomagination" initiative launched by General Electric in 2005 is such an example, potentially raising the bar for other companies. GE is committed to double its R&D investment in developing cleaner technologies, double the revenue from products and services that have significant and measurable environmental benefits and significantly reduce GE's own greenhouse gas emissions.

Third, *weak internal coordination* is another source of reputational risk. When the marketing department of a software company, for instance, launches a large advertising campaign for a new product before developers have identified and ironed out all the bugs, it runs a serious reputational risk. As a result of poor coordination, the firm has initiated their own reputational dilemma by being forced to choose between selling a flawed product and introducing it later than promised. Implementing better corporate governance practices would definitely help to reduce such reputational dilemmas as we will argue in the last chapter.

Building reputation is an investment. From a business perspective, reputation is a credible commitment that sends a strong message to customers and other relevant stakeholders that they can deal with the organizations with confidence. Those crucial stakeholders – especially customers and employees, on top of the usually revered investors – all have certain expectations. When the organization exceeds or matches these different expectations, its corporate reputation usually increases. In that vein, investors will reward firms that perform better than anticipated: its stock price will increase. As mentioned earlier, investors are often treated as the only relevant financial "partners" in a corporation. We like to think that broadening that partnership to customers and employees, and even extending the invitation to the community at large, will help to strengthen the reputation of the firm. That is in essence what the business case of corporate social responsibility attempts to achieve. Link the CSR debate to crisis and reputation risk management, and it is not far fetched to argue that task competence and emotional empathy are the two critical components by which companies are judged during a disaster. The deeper reason for these reactions is directly related to the fact that customers and the public at large come to view the company as a member of the community to live with them, and much less as a legal and rather abstract provider of products and services.[27] Under normal circumstances, companies are engaged in a typically exchange-oriented reciprocal transaction with customers and other stakeholders. However, external disasters and crises often shift the mood of customers and the general public to a more communal orientation, where competence and caring warmth are the prevailing critical success factors for leaders to exude. Wal-Mart's response to provide goods to victims of the Katrina hurricane in the United States in 2005 was a great example where a company superbly prepared, reacted and executed their charity strategy. Not only were their professionals well placed to use the supply management and logistics expertise, but above all, it was the human touch of a caring generous company that made this strategy work. Wal-Mart hugely benefited in terms of social and business reputation.

Once a firm understands which of the three main factors may determine a reputation risk, it still needs to deal with the exact causes of potential reputational damage that is mainly drawn from two sources: outrage and fear.[28] Both are prone to emotional outbursts. One of the reasons why our mistrust in bankers has increased so dramatically just after the outbreak of the financial global crisis in 2008 was the *outrage* of the high remuneration package and the perks that these leaders received while virtually bankrupting the bank. Taking risky bets to invest in toxin-misunderstood derivatives, being well aware that the losses were left to the banks' shareholders and creditors and ultimately to the taxpayer, is not exactly what could be labeled good governance, discharging of fiduciary duties or proper integrated risk management. Of course, it is not so simple to slaughter those executives and boards in the name of presumed justice. However, no one will deny that corporate scandals like the demise of Lehman Brothers in 2008 or the exuberant packages and perks of executives at AIG or Merrill Lynch – while benefiting from a governmental bail out – in the United States or the exuberant remuneration umbrella for top management at the bankrupted Fortis bank in the Benelux are reputation killers. The ensuing outrage drives the crisis. Often, outrage is accompanied by emotions like anger, disgust and contempt, which in turn may trigger desires of revenge or disassociation. Discrimination, for instance, remains one of the most potential triggers of an emotional outrage. Humans have a sensitive and almost hardwired system to sense norm violations; we immediately react to such detection. Moral outrage tends to be derived from intuitive judgments driven by emotions rather than from conscious deliberate reasoning.[29] Moreover, moral outrage frequently triggers a profound desire to take revenge or punish the [alleged] violator, justifying it as a deterrent of future wrong-doing. The Ultimatum Game offers one of the most powerful pieces of evidence for the existence of universal fairness norms.[30] Empirical evidence suggests that the true underlying motive of punishing viola-tors is to exact retribution, even if such punishments carry considerable costs.[31]

Fear is a second source of reputation damage, especially when laypeople evaluate complex risks with which they are unfamiliar. Sometimes fears are based on actual uncertainties; often those fears are fuelled by particu-lar risk perceptions that are not necessarily objectively "true." Emotions and plausible heuristics fuel the perceptions of what we should be afraid of, be it terrorist attacks on airplanes or genetically modified crop. And when laypeople are confronted with complex risks, emotions and easy heuristics simplify the truth behind uncertain phenomena. Fear is often

DOI: 10.1057/9781137547378.0004

an emotional response that frequently does not reflect objective risk, but is triggered by factors like novelty and lack of familiarity, perceived powerlessness, salience of imagination and the danger or becoming the alleged victim of a corporate action.[32]

Indeed, risk perceptions are often about fear, an emotional component that is much less controllable than the rational or cognitive component. Emphasizing the rational component – that is, to what extent is competence and skill able to reduce or prevent events to occur – in risk management is to reduce the hazards as much as possible. However, reacting in a mere competent manner when dealing with emotions that cause reputational risks may even aggravate the dilemma to reduce the tension. As suggested earlier, open and honest communication that is not constrained by prejudice or bias, integrated as part of a cohesive risk management strategy[33] and aligned with the underlying vision/mission, may increase the chances of successfully handling a crisis.

Most reputational challenges do not happen because of some external unfortunate event to materialize, but rather arise as the direct consequence of certain corporate activities that negatively affect stakeholders. Organizations sometimes make decisions without considering the reputational impact of those decisions. In such case organizations and their decision makers – leaders and boards – fail to act as stewards of the corporate reputation.

1.2.2   Reducing reputation risks

Reputation influences the products and services we buy, the investments we make, the job offers we pursue and even the people we choose to be with. We collaborate with others because we trust them, because they have a "good reputation" because they will not consciously or deliberately harm us. There are numerous studies written about the risks and benefits of reputation and the importance of reputation management. A good reputation has a positive effect on the financial bottom line, and the reverse is even more so.

In an economy that becomes more and more knowledge-based, intangible assets such as goodwill and reputation play a considerable role in the valuation of companies. Goodwill accounting and other intangible assets are constituting more than three quarters of the total market capitalization of a number of companies, and for internet-based companies such as Amazon the intangibles rack in to more than 90 percent of the total value of its public traded stock. If something cannot be touched as a tangible asset, such as the value of physical assets, but remains elusive and intangible, the effect of corporate crises can be chilling. It all boils down to trust. And *trust* is possible only where there is a reasonable level of transparency, fairness, accountability and responsibility exercised in the process of delivering products and services.

1.3   Corporate reputation management

Reputation risk is viewed by the majority of executives and investors as the most significant threat posed to a company's global business operations today. However, this reputation risk is much harder to manage than other types of risks, due to its "amorphous" nature as the risk of risks because most risks could have a spillover effect on the public's perception of the company.

Most CEOs admit that their companies lack coordination with respect to who owns reputation risk, and too often responsibilities are hugely fragmented across functions. Moreover, senior executives also find it harder to recover from a reputation failure than to build or maintain reputation. It takes approximately three-and-a-half years for a firm to recover from a reputation failure though firms with a strong reputation (with a proven track record of CSR, for instance) find it easier to recover.[34]

As indicated, reputation risk occurs when a stakeholder's experience with the organization falls below expectations and the stakeholder takes action that negatively impacts the organization's value. First, organizations should clearly define what it is that needs to be known in terms of reputation, followed by identifying and assessing the risk factors that affect reputation. Subsequently, the organization frames how reputation is linked to its branding. It then needs to engage the whole organization in making employees become aware of its vulnerability of reputation and change the culture where appropriate. Leadership then needs to relate the communication programs and customer relationship programs and engage the sales teams to one sound goal that reflects the desired reputation. In other words, organizations need to monitor, identify, assess and manage their reputation risks before they become a crisis.[35] Good effective reputation management strategy will monitor all seven main pillars of corporate reputation and act or react when necessary:

(1) emotional appeal as in trust, admiration and respect; having a vision, providing meaning; (2) quality of management and quality of marketing; (3) products and services expressed in quality, innovativeness, value for money; (4) workplace quality (well-managed, appealing workforce, employee talent, cooperation between teams and among team members); (5) financial performance and financial soundness; (6) social responsibility: community and environmental responsibility; and (7) good corporate governance and wise leadership. Libraries have been written on proper risk management in a variety of industries. In anticipating a reputation issue, it is not that there is no information available, but that too much data is at hand: the challenge is to sift through big data to uncover patterns and reduce the noise. Through proper algorithms and heuristics,[36] data can be turned into useful intelligence and knowledge.

Once potential harmful events or issues have been *identified*, management determines which of those are critical to the company, and which are less crucial. In other words, management subsequently *assesses or evaluates* the reputational magnitude of the potential hazard. In advising boards and top management, we usually warn that anything that can affect a company's value proposition, its core competencies or core values or the company's competitive advantage should be taken seriously. Palm oil companies in Indonesia, for instance, need to assess to what extent illegal logging takes place on their licensed peat land in Sumatra or Borneo to avoid a backlash from their powerful buyers as Unilever, Procter & Gamble and others who themselves are on the watch list of NGOs like Greenpeace. Finally, smart sentiment analysis – often through analyzing social media as will be explained in Chapter 3 – can help management to continuously *monitor* for explosive harmful issues. Knowing that one negative story potentially has a huge impact whereas positive stories have less impact, anticipating or avoiding reputation crisis is far more effective than reacting. Reputation management in its strict sense is a capability developed by top management to go through particular processes of identification, evaluation, monitoring and feedback. Companies will need intelligence systems to prevent risks or to prepare for possible impact.

In a simplified way, we could argue that the basic key areas for measuring and managing reputation are related to (1) what has been told about products/services on the social and digitized media; (2) the organization's desired attributes and associations versus the importance of those attributes and associates to the stakeholder; (3) the stakeholder's expectations of the organization, its industry, or both, versus the experience by the stakeholder; and (4) the stakeholder's experience with the organization, relative to the perceived "ideal" or "best-in-class."

Good reputation management relies not only on vigilance and staying informed, but also on a readiness to respond quickly and effectively to challenges or perceived problems as and when they arise. Such an approach will require that the organization bring together an interdisciplinary team to prepare for online and offline communication strategies. However, whoever the competent executive is on the team, one needs to agree first on what "sticky reputation" is and how it will be measured.[37] In addition, critical for a successful reputation management is that all decision makers view themselves as stewards of the organization's reputation. Concretely, such stewardship implies that the organization integrates the organizational culture, encapsulating the values and beliefs into the processes and strategy of the organization.

Moreover, once a company faces a reputational crisis, the public will not only pay attention to what is happening now, but also to what has been done to prevent it. What we do today prepares our future tomorrow. In general, prevention and preparation are the two main components of reputational management strategies. When Toyota had to recall its cars in 2009 and 2010, critics quickly commented that its aggressive growth strategy had sacrificed quality and safety. Toyota's complaints had been significantly increasing since 2001 but were ignored by its management, or they misinterpreted these warning signs because they were blinded by cognitive biases. They took these near misses as indications that systems were working well, or were not noticing them at all.[38] Hence some strategies can help managers recognize and learn from near misses. In order to avoid or to prevent catastrophes to occur, managers should: (1) be on alert when time or cost pressures are high; (2) watch for deviations from the norm; (3) uncover the deviations' root causes; (4) hold themselves accountable for near misses; (5) envision worst-case scenarios; (6) look for near misses masquerading as successes; and (7) reward individuals for exposing near misses.[39] These strategies aim at reducing the likelihood that such an adverse event will occur. In the inevitable case that external risks cannot be prevented, organizations need to prepare themselves diligently. For instance, data discovery centers need to be built to be in the cloud or somewhere at a safe physical distance in case a natural disaster strikes. So assessing reputational risk requires top management to anticipate and to take proactive steps to *prevent* and to *prepare* for

DOI: 10.1057/9781137547378.0004

possible threatening reputation risks. In addition to a good preparation, successful reputation management almost always requires the ability to swiftly react to unfortunate events and to execute the prepared (crisis or disaster) plan fast and effectively.

And like all risk management processes, we advice top management and boards to follow proven processes and procedures: continuously identify, evaluate and monitor possible risks. And it is not because some of those risks are yet "unknown" today that we can completely ignore them. Black Swans or unexpected high-impact tail risks are extremely dangerous for organizations.[40] Suffice to mention that applying "best practices" could partially help to minimize such risks. Having said that, possible trade-offs or at least potential dilemmas cannot be completely avoided when dealing with reputational challenges: pure financial performance orientation may have a negative impact on the attribute of empathy, for instance, and taking full responsibility for decisions that may help the community may dampen the economic profitability in the short term.

1.3.1 To be a good corporate citizen: balance expertise with empathetic caring

Prudent reputational risk management warns the organization that it may lose control over customer perceptions during a reputational crisis. Mercedes, for instance, introduced the smart A-Class model as the new city car in 1997 with a massive advertising campaign to lure young and female potential customers. Unfortunately, this newly launched A-car had rolled over somewhere in Sweden during a "Moose-test" presentation. Mercedes dismissed this roll-over incident as insignificant and provided expert counterarguments. However, by providing those expert counterarguments, it underestimated the customers' reaction: rather than quickly rebuilding trust, it worsened the crisis. Mere expert assessments can become a dangerous public relations trap. Mercedes was apparently not fully prepared for such a backlash, though they swiftly learnt to get back on their feet, ironically by using an emotional pitch from an expert, Niki Lauda, who lauded the A-Class model as very safe.[41] Preparation strategies to possible crises attempt to mitigate its impact. Often it involves establishing relationships with trusted third parties in advance, upon which the company can fall back in a crisis. Building such relationships takes time, mutual trust and anticipation. Hence a number of big organizations are collaborating with reputable NGOs – trusted by the public – to mitigate potential risks if they would take place. Anticipating possible *strategic* or *external* risks through scenario building, for instance, allows management to become more prudent and to develop tactical steps needed to be undertaken in case the negative (nonpreventable) risk materializes.[42]

Strategically thinking about risks requires the ability to assume an outside perspective and integrate it into the decision making of the organization. The reputational impact of a business decision must be assessed before the decision is effectively made and implemented. In contrast to a crisis situation, during the process of decision making, the stakes are low and the control relatively high, allowing management in that short time period to be proactively prudent and showing necessary foresight. Through decisions today, leaders are preparing the future of the organization. Being caught in a corruption scandal almost always spoils reputation. Corruption is a *preventable* risk that can be avoided by implementing proper standard operating procedures, processes and codes of conduct. When advising boards about the necessity of avoiding corrupt behavior, we often refer to an easy heuristic: how would you feel about a (regrettable) decision if it were accurately reported on the front page of the *Wall Street Journal* or *Financial Times* or a local newspaper? Would that make you feel ashamed or cause guilty feelings? Or would such front page news of alleged corruption not have any significant impact on you, your family or your reputation? Most regret, too late, to be caught up in a corruption scandal.

Reputation and trust clearly show their value when corporations or individuals lose them. In 2006, Siemens was accused of bribing foreign officials to secure contracts abroad. The bribery scandals caused uproar in Germany and beyond. It has seriously tainted Siemens' international reputation. Ultimately, Siemens lost its CEO and chairman in the process, and was shut out from World Bank–financed projects for two years. In addition, Siemens was to pay more than USD 2.6 billion from which USD 1.6 billion were to be paid as fines and fees to the regulators and government officials, and USD 1 billion for internal investigation and reforms.

Leaders and boards are responsible and accountable not only for their own behavior, but also for the behavior of their subordinates. Leadership represents the company; they incarnate the company and impeccable behavior is expected from them as stewards of the company's processes and culture. Some of those crises can lead to "defining moments" that change or subsequently strengthen the culture and values of the organization. The personal integrity of leadership "doing the right thing" should be engrained in the organizational culture and should be beyond questioning. Building and maintaining reputational capital demands leadership and the organization to make the right decisions in their daily operations. Those decisions are usually embedded within a *strategic framework*, tightly connected to core values and its distinctive position in the marketplace. The more core values, purpose and beliefs constitute the organizational culture and its competitive positioning, the clearer the decision making process will be. Because reputation resides in the mind of the public at large, strategically thinking leadership needs to understand and anticipate the *situation* in which outside actors may express opinions. Frequently, reputational challenges are created by outside activists or interest groups who through "private politics"[43] will attempt to force changes in the business practices. Nonetheless, when challenged in the public domain, corporations should not just rely on their expertise and competence, but should show their *empathy* and care for the concerns expressed, and avoid perceived defensive reactions.

As this chapter started referring to the financial institutions that could partially be blamed for the global financial crisis, let us try to apply the notion of reputation risk to the domain of international finance (at Wall Street). How did some financial institutes with less than impeccable ethical behavior lose so much market or stock value at the stock exchange? Reputational risk comprises the risk of loss in the value of a firm's business franchise that extends beyond event-related accounting losses and is reflected in a decline in its share performance metrics. Subsequently, reputation-related losses reflect reduced expected revenues and/or higher financing and contracting costs. The reputational risk in turn is therefore related to the strategic positioning and execution of the firm. Even more so is corporate reputation determined by how leadership and the prevailing culture deal with conflicts of interest exploitation, individual professional conduct, compliance and incentive systems. Reputational risk is often the consequence of management processes rather than discrete events, and therefore requires risk control approaches that differ materially from operational risk. According to this understanding, a reputation-sensitive event – such as attempting to "cook the books" – might trigger an identifiable monetary decline in the market value of the firm. Shareholder value losses in a

DOI: 10.1057/9781137547378.0004

reputation-sensitive situation involve the following sources of losses: (1) client defections and revenue erosion; (2) increases in monetary costs comprising accounting write-offs, associated with the event, increased compliance costs, regulatory fines and legal settlements as well as indirect costs related to the loss of reputation such as higher financing costs, contracting costs and opportunity costs – including "penalty box" suspension by the regulators from particular business activities; and (3) an increases in firm-specific (unsystematic) risk assigned by the market as a result of the reputational event in question.[44] New York University professor Ingo Walter (now visiting at INSEAD), for instance, sees the exploitation of conflicts of interest as one of the key sources of reputational risk in the financial services sector.[45] An additional question, however, is whether these conflicts of interests are *exploited*, imposing specific agency costs on others in the process.[46] In recent years, a number of scholars seem to agree that the role of banks, securities firms, insurance companies and asset managers have become enmeshed in alleged abusive practices, acting simultaneously as principals and intermediaries in a number of high-profile transactions deliberately taking advantage of conflicts of interest.[47]

Mechanisms to control conflicts of interest usually derive from more stringent regulation, possible civil litigation or market discipline. External controls form the basis for a set of internal controls, which can be either prohibitive or affirmative. In the first instance the behavioral "tone" and incentives are established by boards and top management, which aim to steer the loyalty and professional conduct of employees. In other words, these internal control mechanisms are fundamentally matters of sound corporate governance. However, market discipline via reputational impacts on share prices may provide an even more influential and consistent basis for internal defenses against the exploitation of conflicts of interest by financial institutions. The threat of reputational loss may be more effective than (allegedly) complying to regulations or being scared off by the threat of litigation.[48] The reputational loss for misbehavior (exploitation of conflict of interests, for instance) of financial institutions can run up to 66 percent of the total costs, much higher than the accounting write-offs and legal fines.[49] In other words, for each dollar a financial institution at Wall Street attempted to cheat a client or the government, one dollar was paid in legal fees and accounting write-offs, and about 2.6 dollars were lost in stock price decline as the direct result of a reputation loss in the market. Despite the ambiguity of such reputation losses, research by Ingo and Macey conclude that market discipline – fearing for considerable reputation losses – may help to prohibit some unethical and illegal behavior.

It is important that boards and executives look at appropriate metrics that help them to proactively manage or assess reputation risks. Some companies base their entire reputation management program on the yearly beauty contests of *Fortune* "Most Admired" study. As important as these rankings are, they remain a snapshot of reputation in the industries surveyed. These rankings cannot be used or cannot be extrapolated to provide inside knowledge to the company to manage the reputation. One needs to understand the expectation of the value of each of the stakeholder to be able to gain insight into the variables driving reputation. Collaboration between different groups or organizations can be quite useful to mitigate particular reputation risks.

As we argued, corporate reputation is the aggregate of those different perspectives based on these main pillars of corporate performance.

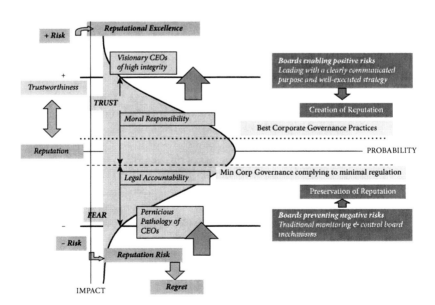

FIGURE 1.1   *The upside opportunity and downside threat on reputation*

Source: A revised interpretation of a framework developed by Verhezen 2009.

DOI: 10.1057/9781137547378.0004

The aggregate for measuring reputation (risk) can be visualized as a reversed Gauss curve – roughly indicating the frequency, impact and probability of (measuring) reputation risks/opportunities to occur – in which leadership aims at optimizing positive risks and minimizing negative risks. As visualized in Figure 1.1, regrettable reputation risks should be avoided, and trustworthy efforts should be made to enhance reputation.50 Good corporate social performance embedded within a philosophy of responsibility can be interpreted as an "insurance policy" against particular reputation risks. Corporate reputation is at stake when trust erodes. Leaders regret often too late to have made a decision that aimed to maximize profits while ignoring the soft side of values and trust within the organization. Internal drivers of values, beliefs, purpose and organizational culture are an effective counterforce to behavior that seek only short-term profitability at all costs.

Notes

1   Diermeier 2011.
2   Diermeier 2011: 32. Corporate reputation is directly linked to the evaluation of core brand attributes. They can affect overall customer perceptions, evaluations of corporate logos and even opinions of product taste and levels of consumption.
3   Bromley 2002.
4   Barnett et al. 2006: 34.
5   Walker 2010: 370. The definitional attributes constituting corporate reputation are perceptual, aggregate and issue specific, comparative, positive or negative and temporal. When measuring corporate reputation, the concerns are reputation for what? And for whom?
6   Fombrun 1996: 78. The three key points of this definition are that (1) it emphasizes the perceptual nature of the construct; (2) it is a net or aggregate perception by all stakeholders, not just one or two; and (3) it is inherently comparative vis-à-vis some standard. What does that mean? Wartik (2002) argues as follows: (1) The empirical truth of corporate reputation comes from whatever the respondents say. Thus, the measurement issues relating to the definition of corporate reputation are only methodological; (2) The definition hardly distinguishes reputation from image and identity, confusing any proper measurement, and the grand aggregation dimension of corporate reputation becomes meaningless since "who is best" could mean for one stakeholder group to another stakeholder group whereas investors may be focused on RoI, for instance. (3) It appears that comparison vis-à-vis some

DOI: 10.1057/9781137547378.0004

standard (past performance, company objective, leading rivals' performance, an industry average, etc.) is sensible to define corporate reputation.

7   Schwaiger 2004; Fombrun 1996, 2007; Dowling 2006b.

8   Bromley 2002; Barnett, Jermier & Lafferty 2006; Walker 2010.

9   De Castro, Lopez & Saez 2006. Corporate reputation covers two components: business and social reputation. Business reputation includes different aspects of corporate reputation that are related to the agents and stakeholders that appear closely tied to the business activities and processes of the firm, as customers, suppliers, managers or employees, whereas social reputation is the result of insights and perceptions of other stakeholders that are not so close to day-by-day business activities, as investors and the community in a wider sense. Business Reputation refers to corporate governance and managerial quality; investment value in the long term; use of corporate assets; innovation level; capability to attract, develop and retain talented people; and product and service quality. Social reputation emphasizes community and social responsibility and financial strength.

10 Younger & Giambona 2011.

11 Walker 2010: 366.

12 Younger & Giambona, 2011.

13 See Sen 2006.

14 Baron 2011, "Goldman Sachs and Its Reputation," Case by Stanford Graduate School of Business Case, distributed by the Case Centre p.77. Goldman Sachs has been perceived as one of the best banks to work for. The basic salary is slightly under the average of other investment banks. Its CEO, for example, makes only USD 600,000 per year, but its bonuses can be enormous. In 2010, the compensation pool at Goldman Sachs was USD 15.3 billion (i.e., 30 percent of the revenues) or USD 450,000 annual bonus compensation for each of the 36,500 employees on average. The CEO Blankfein's bonus fell from USD 68 million in 2007 to "only" USD 9 million in 2009, as a result of the global financial crisis.

15 Fombrun, Gardberg & Sever 2000; Wartick 2002. The reputation quotient is calculated based on 20 attributes in 6 major categories of (1) emotional appeal; (b) products and services; (3) financial performance; (4) social responsibility; (5) vision and leadership; and (6) workplace environment. The results meet most of the characteristics of a solid measure of reputation. The most glaring omission is that only one stakeholder group (i.e., the general public) is the focus. Moreover, Wartick correctly argues that most of these surveys do not have a theoretical framework on which statistical calculations can be made, not statistics as an input into the development of measurement. One needs to understand first what one wants to measure before meaningful statistical analysis can be applied or used *en vogue*.

16 Ponzi, Fombrun & Gardberg 2011. RepTrak Pulse, for instance, is a simplified *emotion-based measure* of corporate reputation and is a potential

measurement tool to (1) assess perceptions of corporate reputation by both the general public and by specialized stakeholders; (2) compare corporate reputation across stakeholders groups; and (3) compare corporate reputation cross-culturally.

17   Reichheld 2006b.

18   In her doctoral thesis (2012, University of Antwerp), Van Den Bogaerd argues that a good reputation will result in better credit availability for firms. Her hypothesis is collaborated by empirical data analysis of firms obtaining better credit conditions through positive media coverage that resulted in a good reputation. Since reputation is built through consistent behavior, firms with a favorable reputation on key attributes are perceived to own capabilities that generate predictable patterns of behavior and performance. As such, reputation serves as a rational and analytical frame for stakeholders, allowing to derive estimates of future behavior of these firms. The institutional perspective on reputation, however, tends to focus more on a general, affective characteristic of corporate reputation, with reputation being characterized as a global impression representing how a collective perceives a firm. Institutionalists portray reputation as an interaction between information exchanges and social influence among various actors interacting in an organizational field. In this vein, reputation reflects prominence or the collective awareness and recognition that an organization has accumulated.

19   Walker 2010. If the attributes of corporate reputation are perceptual, aggregate and issue specific, comparative, positive or negative, and temporal, then we can argue that the perception of internal stakeholders as communicated in the organizational identity, aligned and combined to the perception of external stakeholders and expressed in the organizational image result in a corporate reputation.

20   In Kiel 2015: 98.

21   Pentland 2008, 2014. Yet sociometric data have shown that unconscious processes and tacit knowledge are potentially even more important in determining the behavior of organizations and their leaders, and subsequently their reputation.

22   Porter & Kramer 2006, 2011.

23   Klewes & Wreschniok, 2011.

24   During a dinner with professor Ed Freeman – one of the "founders" of the Stakeholder Theory – at the Melbourne Business School in August 2010, we had a lengthy discussion on the socioeconomic costs of the Shareholder Theory while acknowledging that there is enormous overlapping between the two presumed antagonistic models. It was then that Ed Freeman suggested to switch the notion of "shares" (or stocks) with "stakes" that would make the real benefit and costs of good stakeholder management more obvious.

DOI: 10.1057/9781137547378.0004

Everyone who is in one form or another committed or linked to the company has a direct or indirect stake in the company and will be able to affect the value of the company. Hence the importance of recognizing these "stakes," which in my opinion are directly linked to how reputation is formed and constructed.

25 Ang & Wight 2009.

26 Eccles, Newquist & Schatz 2007.

27 Diermeier 2011; Larkin 2003.

28 Diermeier 2011 provides an excellent analysis of reputational damage as a consequence of outrage and fear in the context of business.

29 Green 2013; Diermeier 2011; Pfaff 2015.

30 Klein 2014; Green 2013. Although the violation of fairness norms triggers moral outrage and a desire for retribution, the exact content of fairness norms varies by culture.

31 Green 2013; Haidt 2012.

32 Diermeier 2011: 167–170. Promising technologies frequently encounter resistance and never are able to reach the full potential. Fear based on opinion rather than experience and facts is the main factor in such situations. Different applications of the same technology can differ dramatically in terms of their potential to create fear. The example of Monsanto is revealing. Critics have attributed Monsanto's failure to get their genetically modified good accepted in Europe to arrogance, and an exclusive focus on the scientific aspects of the its products. But another reason was that Monsanto essentially employed the same strategic approach in Europe as it did in the growth hormone case in the United States: the use of government regulators as trusted third parties. But this approach assumed that regulators enjoy similar levels of trust in other countries, which is not the case. Government agencies rank near the bottom in terms of credibility in Europe, whereas NGOs (criticizing Monsanto) are well trusted in an European context. The goal is to collaborate with those trusted parties that have the highest credibility in the given market. So by using government agencies, Monsanto inadvertently targeted the "wrong" credible group and underestimated the power of the NGOs in Europe, which are less credible in the United States.

33 Larkin 2003.

34 Conference Board USA 2010.

35 Schreiber, 2011. The process of monitoring, identifying, assessing and managing risks is about preparing for possible crises and preventing them. Having proper processes in place allows organizations to differentiate between rational (and reasonable) approaches to risk assessment and to avoid rationalizing risks. However, because the risks can occur anywhere, inside or outside the organization, one needs a structure in place that can

DOI: 10.1057/9781137547378.0004

become the "eyes and ears" of the organization, with multiple stakeholders and multiple touch points.

36   Pink 2009: 27. When facing complexity, one needs to distinguish whether the challenge can be resolved through algorithms or heuristics. An "algorithmic task is one in which you follow a set of established instructions down a single pathway to one conclusion. That is, there is an algorithm for solving it. A heuristic task is the opposite. Precisely because no algorithm exists for it, you have to experiment with possibilities and devise a novel solution." Almost all creative novel solutions require the use of both the left analytical and right intuitive brain, with an emphasis on the latter.

37   Sticky reputation is an interesting notion used by the researchers Schultz, Mouritsen and Gabrielsen (2001) to criticize sloppily defined reputational surveys – beauty contests as we labeled them – because they conclude that (1) the ranking usually cannot discriminate finely between the criteria they are asked to quantify; (2) the more general markers of firms' achievements may relate to their size and not necessarily to the attributes and variables constituting reputation over time; (3) the majority of the sticky firms are also companies that seem able to adapt to the new societal expectations as to legitimate corporate behavior, with social responsibility and concern for the environment being the most obvious areas; and (4) sticky reputation may also reflect the firm's ability to imitate or adapt to new institutional albeit fashionable demands, generating the formal structures and communicative rituals needed to obtain a minimum level of legitimacy, and thus "reputation."

38   Tinsley, Dillon & Madsen 2011.

39   Tinsley, Dillon & Madsen 2011: 93 & 97. The authors argue that
Cognitive biases make these near misses hard to see, and, even when they are visible, leaders tend not to grasp their significance. Thus, organizations often fail to expose and correct latent errors even when the cost of doing so is small – and so they miss opportunities for organizational improvement before disaster strikes. This tendency is itself a type of organizational failure – a failure to learn from "cheap" data. Surfacing near misses and correcting root causes is one the soundest investments an organization can make.

40   See Taleb 2004 & 2007.

41   Diermeier 2011.

42   Kaplan & Mikes 2012.

43   A term we borrow from Dr. D. Diermeier from Kellog's Business School.

44   Walter 2006. Professor Ingo Walter describes how manipulation of accounting at Wall Street resulted in significant financial losses for those companies caught, with the majority of the lost value due to reputation risk.

45   Walter 2006: 21. Citigroup, for instance, has been engaged in the pursuit of revenue economies of scope (what is labeled as cross-selling), while simultaneously targeting both the asset and liability sides of its client's balance sheet. Concretely, it meant that Citibank was generating advisory

DOI: 10.1057/9781137547378.0004

fee income, managing assets and meeting the private banking needs of WorldCom's CEO. That success (of cross-selling) resulted in conflicts of interest relating to retail investors, institutional fund managers, WorldCom executives and shareholders as well as Citigroup's own positions in WorldCom credit exposure and stock trades. WorldCom's bankruptcy triggered a large market capitalization loss for Citigroup's own shareholders, only part of which can be explained by a $2.65 billion civil settlement the firm reached with investors in May 2004.

46   We note that the exploitation of conflict-of-interests requires some form of information asymmetry and market frictions. Obviously, this conflict of interest exploitation is sensitive to the strategic positioning of the financial institution, as well as the performance pressure imposed on individual business units and individuals. Nonetheless appropriate conflict of interest diagnostics and better good corporate governance can promote sensible safeguards against the reputational exposure involved.

47   Roubini 2011; Shiller 2012; Walter 2006; Rajan 2011; Admati & Hellwig 2013; Taft 2015.

48   Yale professor Macey postulates the hypothesis (2013) that corporate reputation was the unifying power to keep partnerships ethical at Investment Companies like Goldman Sach and JP Morgan and many others. However, when those equity partnerships went public, and turned into limited liability companies, the cohesion of individual reputation of each of the partners swiftly evaporated since maximizing profitability – shareholder value – became the main criterion of success, and corporate reputation within the group started to play a much less significant role.

49   Walter 2006.

50   As we search for meaning in our careers, a good guide to use is to face and accept reality that is usually complex and rather ambiguous, use Occam's razor and simplify. Einstein told us to make things as simple as possible, but not simpler. We cannot change who we are and what we are given nor can we change the past. But we can always act and live in the present to shape our future.

DOI: 10.1057/9781137547378.0004

2
Reputation under Direct and Indirect Reciprocity

Abstract: *Repeated encounters as in direct reciprocity between the same individuals engender trustworthy behavior. However, under indirect reciprocity where people do not necessarily often meet each other, relationships and exchanges are built on the reputation of those participants. In others words, thanks to the power of reputation, we are willing to be involved with others or help others without expecting an immediate return. It seems that we ll behave less selfish when we know that we live in the shadow of the future, as expressed in our reputation. Having a good reputation carries quite some benefits for businesses or individuals.*

Verhezen, Peter. *The Vulnerability of Corporate Reputation: Leadership for Sustainable Long-Term Value*. Basingstoke: Palgrave Macmillan, 2015. DOI: 10.1057/9781137547378.0005.

The pursuit of financial gain leads to predatory behavior and pure exploitation by certain powerful groups, especially when short-term profitability is the result of one-off "noniterative" transactions by traders – acting as renters rather than real owners – that maximizes zero-sum calculations of self-advantage.[1] However, certain mechanisms favor collaboration and sharing (perceived) information that help organizations to thrive. In order to survive as a thriving cluster, organizations require mechanisms and structures that coordinate action and prevent exploitation from within to remain vigilant and competitive for outsiders. It is the evolutionary mechanisms of *direct and indirect reciprocity* that includes *reputation* as a criterion to enable organizations to structure themselves to fit the environment in the most suitable and effective manner. This is especially true in an era of a new evolving Internet of Things and increasingly connected society or networked Commons.[2]

2.1   Champions of good reputation

Being a good corporate citizen usually results in obtaining a good corporate reputation in the eyes of those who could affect the for-profit organization. Being perceived as a generous and/or empathetic corporate citizen who does not financially perform will not last though. Champions are those enterprises that perform financially and are able to align those economic objectives to social-ecological yardsticks that are increasingly gaining importance in the eyes of customers, employees and the community at large. The hypothesis is that such alignment of business and social values is possible when clusters of organizations in the supply chain are able to establish some close collaboration. Some would speak of "blended value," others prefer to describe it as "corporate citizenship" or "stewardship" or "corporate shared value". Or, we shall simply label it "corporate responsibility."

2.1.1   Conditional "generosity" or selfish "taking"? What strategic choice to make?

In purely zero-sum situations and win-lose interactions, giving generously or acting altruistically rarely pays off. However, life in general and organizational life in particular is not zero-sum; on balance, people employees and executives who choose giving or cooperating as their primary "reciprocity" style end up reaping benefits and rewards. Wharton Business School professor Grant provocatively states that his research indicates that the most "competitive" and worst performers in

DOI: 10.1057/9781137547378.0005

business are those who give their time and share their resources; in other words, a clear link seems to exist between reciprocity styles and business success. Givers dominate the bottom and the top of the success ladder in business. Those in the middle – the "matchers" and "takers" – where those who calculated and only gave when it was clear that the other party would reciprocate. Such an attitude of merely taking or calculated reciprocity was clearly based on a rather selfish *do ut des* policy.[3] Successful "givers" are as ambitious as "takers" and "matchers" but they simply have a different more generous and apparently more effective style to pursue their goals. Indeed, "givers are more likely to become champs – not only chumps.[4]" Apparently, the most competent and competitive executives were those who did give, but conditionally, and who developed huge networks on which they could rely on. In other words, those top executives who conditionally give – precluding waste and being taken advantage of – stretched their time horizons out far enough to create social capital. Network or social capital allows building links whereby one needs to distinguish strong ties of our close friends and family and those we really trust from weak ties of acquaintances or people we know casually.[5] Strong ties provide bonding and protection. Surprisingly, people looking out for a new job relied much more on weak ties than on strong ties: 28 percent heard about a new job from a weak tie, which serves as a bridge, providing more efficient access to new information.[6] It is "givers" who have a distinctive edge over "takers" and "matchers" in unlocking dormant ties that are often neglected in our networks. They seem to be much more efficient in being able to use those weak network ties or social capital because of the trust they have created over time and which seems to function as genuine capital they can rely on or fall back on.[7] As argued earlier, most people are matchers and takers; their core values focus on fairness, equality and reciprocity. When takers violate these principles, matchers in their networks believe in "an eye for an eye" by having justice served, acting as "karma police." Again, Evolutionary and Game Theory help us to value the importance of reciprocity and survival as groups through enlightened self-interest. And that is where reputation plays a neat role: in networks. Givers see interdependence as a source of strength, a way to create a greater good in the organization as a consequence of close(r) collaboration of the group members achieving a "greater good". If such collaboration succeeds to expand the pie, both the groups as well as the givers who are instrumental in the improvement will benefit.[8] Givers will collaborate with those who do not take advantage or who are possibly willing to reciprocate in the future.

DOI: 10.1057/9781137547378.0005

Teamwork embedded in an innate paradigm of reciprocity is the signature adaptation of organisms in human and organizational evolution.

Obviously, it takes time and effort for givers to build goodwill and trust, but eventually, they establish relationships and reputations that enhance their success. Reputation helps them to increase their "shadow" of good behavior. Giving in order to get a better reputation in the eyes of other stakeholders takes time. It may not be the "optimal" approach for sprinters whose time horizon is very short term, but it definitely is valuable if one is participating in a marathon. And organizational life looks more like a marathon than a sprint. Moreover, with an increasingly important and expanding service sector in Europe and the United States and other developed countries, as well as in emerging countries, more and more people and stakeholders will place a premium on providers who have established relationships and reputations as "givers" and not just "takers." In any community, collaboration and cooperation is crucial to survive and to thrive. However, the fear of being judged as weak or naive in business by peers prevents many executives from operating like givers at work. Such unfortunate behavior results in suboptimal solutions, as the Prisoner's Dilemma (PD) and the subsequent Nash equilibrium have proven.[9] Moreover, the Cornell economist Robert Frank suggests that encouraging people to expect the worst in others apparently brings out the worst in people[10] as in a self-fulfilling prophesy. Nonetheless, what this chapter tries to demonstrate is that success in business does not need to be at someone else's expense.

Having lived in Asia Pacific for half of my life, I have learnt the importance of creating and sustaining relationships and of building business networks where other people can get deals and benefit from our relationships. Admittedly, it may not immediately bring personal benefits. But a "good reputation of being a trustworthy partner" is professionally rewarding, especially over a longer period. Call it the law of "karma" where causal reciprocity and the mechanism of reputation play their important function. Moreover, it creates a world I prefer to live in. The counterintuitive proposition is therefore that relationships benefit directly or indirectly from a "pragmatic altruistic" or cautious generous attitude. By setting up a situation to help others without immediately or directly financially benefiting, we rapidly reinforce our own reputation and expand our own possibilities. What goes around comes around.

Let us think about the following two examples. First, Mittal's Bharti Enterprises, the parent company of Bharti Airtel – a global telecom

DOI: 10.1057/9781137547378.0005

giant – had grown fast over the past decade. But around 2011–2012, cash became tight at the company because of slower than expected growth in Africa (where Bharti Airtel had heavily invested) and external regulatory changes. In addition, interest and inflation were on the rise in India, the rupee lost value and the company struggled to service/pay back its debt. Some befriended investment bankers helped the company get the financing it needed to go through this rough spot, without falling in the nepotistic trap. It was Mittal's reputation of being a savvy and reliable businessman and his relationships that proved to be as valuable as cash in dealing with these uncertainties.[11] Our second example refers to Pri Notowidigdo[12] who founded and still manages Amrop Indonesia, a boutique executive research company. He is known as a very professional "headhunter" and mentor to many people. What makes him so unique is his willingness to genuinely value the person he helps to place in executive or board seats. He has an incredible international business network that is based on respect and the tacit understanding that we always need to be ready to help where appropriate. Obviously, this empathetic "giver" has an impeccable reputation that has significantly helped his business over the years. People, partners and competitors alike trust Pri; he is honest and known to be reliable.

Others will judge us in these networks and bestow good or bad reputation on us. Paradoxically, the phenomenon of *gossip* helps to build such a reputation. Gossip is a way of enticing nonrelated individuals – which can be even extended to "credible organizations" – into cooperation that benefits both. As unpleasant as gossip can be, it enables a new form of cooperation and sometimes even selflessness: if I help a stranger, it can pay off if others witness this deed allowing me to be perceived as trustworthy since these others will start talking about this deed, as in gossip. As long as society considers helping others as something good and thus as a sign of trustworthiness, these deeds of cooperative behavior – and in its extreme, a gesture of generosity – would be perceived as a normative yardstick in our society where trading and exchange has become crucial. Indeed, in order to function, markets need a minimal form of trust – and preferably some form of sanction to penalize violators of this trust – without which the exchanges between economic trading partners would seize to exist. Moreover, anthropological studies reveal that humans spend 65 percent of their conversation talking about the bad and good deeds of other people; call it *gossiping*. Well, people seem to almost naturally get into gossiping because it reinforces a social control system to improve cooperation, a proven better way to

DOI: 10.1057/9781137547378.0005

survive in groups. Indeed, not only do people gossip easily, it seems to happen automatically. And strangely enough, not gossiping requires great effort.[13] We are social animals to the core.[14] It seems that gossip constitutes popular knowledge that allows trust to develop. Those who violate our trust will get their reputation tainted because people punish them by sharing reputational information. *Gossip* represents a widespread, efficient and low-cost form of punishment, or a useful way to inform others about a person about whom information is not readily available. Gossip is a loose form of reputational information. And when people have access to this reputational information, it becomes obvious how one is treated in their respective networks. And the internet makes this timeless. Since relationships and reputations are visible to the world through e-networks, it has become much harder to get away with fake or inappropriate behavior; in other words, achieving "sustainable" success as a "taker" has become much harder in these times of transparency and increased scrutiny, anywhere any time.

A minimum level of generosity for individuals and the threat of retaliation by organizations allow collaboration to materialize, optimizing the equilibrium or improving the economic outcomes.[15] In addition, in cases of uncertain and overly asymmetric information between participants, reputation will allow these leaders to take favorable decisions. Similarly, business leaders and stakeholders will use reputation as "money" under uncertain circumstances. And in an increasingly connected world, the gossip about organizations and their leaders in social media cannot be underestimated. Reputation and trustworthiness are factors that constitute "survival," or at least prolong a healthy organizational life.

Admittedly, reciprocity is a powerful norm, but the downside is that information about a person or organization can be manipulated, or that the information itself could be incorrect or untruthful. Gossip about someone does not always necessarily reflect the real facts or truth of the matter; gossip is often and purposely misinterpreted, or even made up to deliberately damage a person's reputation.

2.1.2 How to resolve the tragedy of commons and Prisoner's Dilemma?

Business and (neo)classical economics assume that we all act like rational self-interest individuals who would undertake all endeavors to maximize our own benefit and those of our kin. In Evolutionary and

Game Theory, it is often referred to as the Tragedy of Commons[16] and the PD.[17] Today, this tragedy (of commons) has regained prominence again as pollution, for instance, has been the immediate result of an overuse of particular ingredients by quite a number of organizations that have severely damaged our environment, a common good,[18] and the reputation of those causing the (social) harm. In our internet linked economy, the "commons" approach to collaborate seem to gain track.[19]

An attitude of (conditional) generosity will likely result in a more prudent use of resources since long-term sustainability would be high on the list of an "empathetic" corporate citizen. Interestingly, the late Nobel Prize winner for Economics, Elinor Ostrom, has argued that groups (of organizations) could avoid the tragedy of overuse, assuming that they adhere to or respect certain self-regulating design principles, among which are an understanding of clear purpose to coordinate activities, a monitoring system with graduated sanction where necessary, and an adapted governance mechanism with conflict resolution.[20] The economic wisdom here demonstrates that groups are able to manage their own affairs without top-down regulation or the necessity of privatizing the resources or assets as long as these groups know how to collaborate with each other without undermining the common good objective. In Bali, farmers have learnt over centuries to share water for their rice paddy fields through an ingenious cascade water system that no one has been able to copy yet. This old traditional innovative water system relies on symbolic capital (in being perceived as trustworthy individuals who collaborate) and whose "joint" reputation is interlinked to social capital (or a network of farmers within a community that exercises peer pressure). This cascade water system has proven to generate above-average economic results, which is the definition of having a good strategy that results in excess cash above the industry average. Organizations as living organisms can therefore "defend" themselves against actions that benefit some individual (or organization) at the expense of others within the group. The reputation mechanism allows organizations or a group within an organization to coordinate activities to achieve common goals.

The PD, on the contrary, is a powerful mathematical visualization of a struggle of the individual person (or organization) and the collective good. Cooperation results in an optimal equilibrium under the PD, whereas mere self-interest almost always leads to suboptimal solutions.[21] In a competitive environment, one has good reasons to cooperate when the benefit is larger than the cost, which is the crux of the PD.[22] However, most people will act selfishly against the best interest of the organizational or common good. Similarly, organizations will optimize their own shareholder value even if that would be at the expense of (an investment in) a better product or a more sensible common good solution. The most one can apparently expect is that individuals or organizations will protect their kin, their own members of the family against outsiders. In other words, only when we are sure that some of our own, be it genes or a family member, will benefit, one acts generously.[23] By extension, "living" organizations will also act in their own interest, by maximizing the interest of their "owners," and "kill off" competition where needed or necessary. The PD, indeed, reveals us that competition and hence conflict are always present in life. Counterintuitively, competition can sometimes lead to cooperation to become more adapted to the challenges in a global context. And for that to happen, one will need to rely on the mechanism of reputation that helps organizations to cooperate in order to achieve a "higher" more sustainable goal.

Although mutual cooperation can be proven to lead to a higher payoff than mutual defection or free-riding, people who would decide to be "rational" and therefore self-interested may opt for short-term benefits at the expense of the group, which ultimately harms themselves. Cooperation seems to be irrational in the short term. Contrary to this apparent obvious hypothesis – on which most of neoclassical economics is based to maximize short-term profitability – experimental game theory, however, more often than not indicates that individuals do not necessarily pursue selfish rational behavior but do act cooperatively. Indeed, in PD situations, individuals often try to cooperate; only when they learn that it does not work do they switch to selfish "defection." In other words, (1) when individuals engage in repeated encounters as in *direct reciprocity* that creates trust based on previous actual behavior, or (2) when they have tools to rely on *reputational information* about individuals or groups, cooperation makes a chance to prevail. "Tomorrow never dies":[24] history has a beginning but it has no end. It is this *shadow of the future*, as in the reputation of someone, that makes people more reliable to cooperate because of the negative impact or sanctions it may have when being caught for cheating the other individual or group. It is the mechanism of reputation that drives the behavior of those individuals, especially in cases where one does not have direct access to information about

DOI: 10.1057/9781137547378.0005

the individual. In the same way, the reputation "or the trustworthiness" of an organization will affect how the entity is treated by other stakeholders who can definitely affect the value of the organization by customers boycotting products or government issuing stringent regulations stifling creativity.

Similarly, competition between individuals seems to favor egocentrism, while competition between groups favors selflessness or (prudent) altruism of its individual members.[25] So far we have argued that there exists enough reasons for individuals to engage in benevolent collaboration or prudent altruism within groups or organizations. It may result in corporate citizenship behaving properly and empathetically as long as it provides a competitive advantage. We did not resolve yet to explain why it might be beneficial as well to establish collaboration between organizations to address global (common good) challenges. First, we will argue how collaboration between groups and individuals could be possibly brought to a more global level; subsequently, we explain how to protect against free-riders and cheaters, and how the (access to) internet is fundamentally changing our attitude, emphasizing the importance of trustworthiness, sharing and transparency.

2.2 Parable of organizational evolution and the function of reputation

Business seems to be based on fierce competition between organizations rewarding selfish and competitive behavior. Nonetheless, humans are the champions of cooperation. And yes, the best performing business organizations are those that have managed to increase their internal cooperation within the firm.[26]

Adam Smith's Invisible Hand may need some strong amendments to remain relevant for economics. Without the strong social ties – characterizing Adam Smith's temporal context in which bourgeois residents knew each other almost personally – capitalism can easily turn rapacious. In our contemporary interconnected economic world, most ties are weak and all too often the invisible hand may no longer function as it apparently did. Only when we understand how socioeconomic collaborative interactions work together with competitive forces can we hope to ensure some kind of peaceful stability and social fairness in our networked society. Communities are made up of social ties, and without the constraints of social pressure and reputational risk provided by social ties, the capitalist mechanism can become quite predatory.

2.2.1   Repetitive business exchanges favor those with a good reputation

Individuals within the group of an organization will easier collaborate with close mates and friends than with people they don't know. Such individuals' selfish genes will collaborate because it is in their own advantage to progress to do so. Empathy among friends and family members seems to be rather easy to apply. Nonetheless, individuals also collaborate with nonfamily members as long as this is beneficial.

When people repeatedly need to collaborate with other team members of a group, team members will continue to collaborate till the other member would "defect" or "cheat": a *Tit-for-Tat strategy*[27] has proven to be quite resilient in joining forces to improve competitiveness. In other words, such repetition creates a kind of trust between those team members and enhances the chances of joint collaboration that benefits these individuals or team members. On average, a Tit-for-Tat strategy is very successful at inducing cooperation. However, its weakness lies in the inability to deal with errors or (un)conscious mistakes to cheat in repeated PD that result in low pay-offs. In other words, in case individuals make the "mistake" to free-ride or to opt to commit a selfish act, it will lead to suboptimal solutions[28] because tit-for-tat will follow such selfish behavior undermining any optimal long-term solution or result. Instead, forgiving your partner will result in better solutions over a longer time period; such strategy is called a *Generous Tit-for-Tat* (GTfT). The danger, however, exists that members with the reputation to follow a GTfT strategy could be exploited by less generous members. How to resolve that dilemma?

Mere generosity or altruism[29] is, indeed, not optimal over a longer period because a group of cooperating altruists can be easily invaded and manipulated by more selfish individuals. Hence instead of always unconditionally giving or always collaborating with team members, those individuals who applied a more measured approach of GTfT will likely survive better. Trust plays a crucial role in sustaining such cooperation between individuals. Such trustworthiness will increase a sense of community within the group, strengthening its "survival instinct."

DOI: 10.1057/9781137547378.0005

Indeed, common ground is a major influence in explaining cooperative and generous giving behavior leading to "supercooperators."[30] When people share an identity with another person, giving to or cooperating with that person takes on an "otherish"[31] or caring empathetic quality. Helping people within our own group equals helping ourselves as we are making the group better off. It is this identification and cohesion within organizational groups that explains cooperative behavior in such groups based on trust between their members.

Individuals are motivated to care and to give to others when they identify – though not all necessarily in an equal manner – as part of a common community, say a commitment to a particular group within the organization. The paradox though is that people have a strong desire to fit in, to strive for connection, cohesiveness, community and affiliation with other group members, while at the same time, individuals want to stand out, to be different and unique. That explains why individuals prefer to work for organizations with a reputation of being unique that stands out. Global brands Google and Apple, or smaller local firms like Torfs Shoes in Belgium, are just three examples of companies that are able to attract talented employees who care since the company seem to care for them. Groups or organizations that share unique similarities attract such strong-minded individuals, facilitating bonding and thus the chances of competitive survival. The same applies to group sports where championship-winning teams almost always have shifted from individual showmanship to teamwork, or from "taking" to "giving."

However, taking into account that *GTfT* can drift to unconditional cooperation, it in turn invites defectors who will selfishly take advantage and undermine the cooperation. Hence the optimal solution would be a kind of careful cooperation that implies possible sanctioning or "revenge" systems to punish potential or would be selfish distractors. According to Harvard professor Martin Nowak, the best sustainable strategy is a *win-stay lose-shift* approach that is safeguarding cooperation but sanctioning any deliberate defective uncooperative behavior.[32] Unconditional – and according to Nowak, defenseless – cooperators tend to be exploited.[33] Intuition teaches us that organizations that are too nice will not sustain in a competitive environment. *So both extremes of mere niceness to all stakeholders for the sake of achieving community goals or mere selfish unreliable corporate behavior – that can loosely be translated into selfish shareholder maximizing organizations – will not be the winners at the end of the day. It is the companies with the reputation of being trustworthy and those that do take*

DOI: 10.1057/9781137547378.0005

into account the stakeholders' concerns that will be financial winners while having succeeded to align business to societal objectives. Call it applied PD cases into the real world! Empirical data seem to confirm that champions in business are those CEOs and their companies that create high return on investment for their shareholders while simultaneously embracing social and environmental objectives.[34]

From an evolutionary perspective, it is not too difficult to argue that all our cooperative teamwork[35] and current collaboration between organizations have evolved for the purpose of successful "survival" in the competition of using limited resources in the most effective or, shall we say, most profitable way. Cooperation between groups and organizations has been used as competitive weapons, as a strategy to outcompeting other organizations or to maximize their own profitability. However, it may be worth considering about a next step in the evolution of organizational cooperation in an increasingly "sharing" and *digitized* (global) economy in which transaction costs have significantly fallen. Some healthy competition can weed out inefficient and too expensive activities, while collaboration between organizations may lead to address some of the more global and thus "beyond-tribal"[36] socioeconomic challenges.

From a strategic perspective, we believe that in the today's crowded market, the best way to create a clear differentiation is to establish an *experiential ecosystem*[37] that creates and delivers (customer and employee) value – beyond just the organizational own product, and that ultimately results in superior financial performance, as in superior shareholder or investor value. Creating and maintaining such an ecosystem requires collaboration with other organizations. And yes, less well-adopted or inefficient firms will be doomed to disappear in the process of competition to succeed and to survive. But to the surprise of most economists and businesses, that competitive contest may not necessarily be won by selfish-oriented merely profit-seeking firms, but rather by organizations that have learnt to coordinate with others and that have given a meaningful purpose to their employees and customers, while providing a decent return to their investors.

Similarly, in an era of a global neural network – through the ubiquitous Internet – that is designed to be open, distributed and collaborative, everyone will have access to anyone anywhere any time. The rise of collaborative commons[38] – as in a sharing, collaborative economy or even circular economy – through the Internet of Things is ultimately based on trust, or social capital where reputation plays its role. Be it at

DOI: 10.1057/9781137547378.0005

eBay, Amazon, Airbnb, Uber or Kickstarter, the focus is more on access than on ownership.

2.2.2   Trust under direct reciprocity and reputation under indirect reciprocity

Direct reciprocity is fundamental in any interexchange as we know in business or social life.[39] Such reciprocity is based on repetitive encounters between individuals generating trust[40] that can lead to some form of cooperation if it enhances the group's success. Or, if the probability of another encounter between two individuals (of the same group, for instance) exceeds the cost-to-benefit ratio of this altruistic or generous cooperative behavior, one can expect them to continue to cooperate.[41] Direct reciprocity that engenders trustworthy behavior relies on repeated encounters between the same individuals, often within a group. Trust as a form of empathy is the willingness to cooperate with another before monitoring his performance, perhaps even without any capability ever to monitor it. Trust is the willingness to give discretionary power, to postpone checking and accounting. Therefore trust is accepted *vulnerability* to another, possibly but not expected ill will (or lack of goodwill) toward one.[42] In other words, risk is of the very essence of trust. Trust is morally preserved by truthfulness and trustworthiness.

What about individuals of a particular group helping another individual outside this group whom he might not meet anymore? In other words, what about collaboration under *Indirect reciprocity*? For direct reciprocity one seems to need a "*face*" whereas for indirect reciprocity one needs a "name," as in relying on someone's reputation. A name implies communication about that individual or organization. In such a situation, an individual will care or help or assist another individual when it will benefit his reputation. While direct reciprocity relies on the direct experience and thus trustworthiness of repeated encounters or exchange between individuals or organizations, indirect reciprocity takes into account the experience of other people. My behavior toward the other depends on what the other has done to others. We all are aware that societies and groups or organizations within those societies have evolved as trustworthy parties despite the increased complexity. It has been the mechanisms of reputation that allows citizens or businesses to undertake exchanges even with those with whom one never has done business. Thanks to the power of reputation we are willing to be involved

DOI: 10.1057/9781137547378.0005

with others or to help others without expecting an immediate return. More, we are willing to take the initiative to cooperate or help others in (or as) an organization because we are well aware that this act will boost the chance of being helped by someone else in the future. We all behave more socially or less selfishly when we know that we live in *the shadow of the future*.

Let us try to prove our point of indirect reciprocity and its reputation mechanism with a by now infamous example.[43] Google was incorporated by someone with good reputation who brought different parties together. When Larry Page and Sergey Brin were seriously pondering over the possibility to take Google commercial beyond the subject of their PhD at Stanford, they reached out to Stanford professor David Sheriton who himself could be described as a (conditional) "giver," top academic and an entrepreneur himself. It was on David's veranda that the young entrepreneurs Larry Page and Sergey Brin were introduced to Andy Von Bechtolsheim – who had bought one of David Sheriton's companies before. Andy's reputation in Silicon Valley – he was one of the founders of Sun Microsystems, among others – was beyond doubt of princeling status. The presentation by Page and Brin impressed Andy Von Bechtolsheim so much that the same evening he paid them a cheque of USD 100,000, urging them to incorporate this brilliant idea of a search engine into a real venture. Because of Von Bechtolsheim's impeccable reputation, and the rumor that he was backing up these two young researchers Page and Brin, consequently resulted in two competing Silicon Valley investors Sequoia and Kleiner Perkins joining to back up this new venture; Google Inc. was born, and the rest is history. Google can be delightfully described as the direct result of collaboration on all levels. First, the search engine itself is the symbiosis between machine and human. Indeed, the search engine embeds the usage of human wisdom – which independently developed numerous websites with certain intentions to link it to particular audiences – into an automated algorithm that provided online information wherever and whenever. Google has automated the process of making linkages and giving priorities in a superior manner. Google intends to facilitate the collaboration between humans and machines in such a way that abundant or even excessive data can be organized into accessible information and meaningful intelligence, and ultimately into useful knowledge. And, the incorporation of Google was the result of indirect reciprocity, based on the mechanism of reputation.

DOI: 10.1057/9781137547378.0005

Research has proven that individuals (and by extension organizations) who are more helpful and more importantly who have established a reputation of being helpful and generous are more likely to receive help and assistance when asked or needed.[44] Most likely, indirect reciprocity has also led to the evolution of moral and social norms, promoting cooperation that enhances the group's or individual's survival. Indirect reciprocity can therefore promote cooperation between individuals or groups if the probability to know someone's reputation exceeds the cost-to-benefit ratio of the generous or altruistic act,[45] which is made easier in these days of internet scrutiny and "gossiping." Moreover, cooperators – whether individuals or groups – form network clusters where they are feeling safer to help each other and not being manipulated by free-riding outsiders.[46] In addition, groups can impose direct or indirect sanctions for not collaborating or for free-riding or manipulating the group's generosity.[47] Concretely, exposing someone's negative reputation may be a very effective way to redirect its behavior to a more civil and conscious one. Indeed, the prospect of vengeful retaliation seems to pave the way for amicable cooperation.[48] It is worth noting that transgressions of agreed cooperation do not require heavy-handed punishment or revenge, at least initially. We are all familiar that a gentle reminder or even gossip is sufficient, whereas the danger of more severe forms of punishment is waiting in the wings for use if deemed necessary.[49]

Is it true that humans do coordinate better when under duress or under threat? How does punishment fit into this story of cooperation? Researchers Feher and Gaechter coined the term "altruistic punishment,"[50] indicating that people are willing to punish others for the greater good, even when they do not immediately benefit from it. Indeed, these two economists have argued that punishment might be a powerful force to promote cooperation between individuals.

However, in other studies, best performing teams never used punishment.[51] In contrast, the worst performing individuals used punishment most often.[52] Could one argue that winners do not punish, but losers do? It looks like that rewards function better to motivate individuals to perform than punishments. However, when cooperation to perform is in peril, potential sanctions could deter free-riders or defection to cheat. When individuals are already disengaged and about to undermine collaboration in the organization, punishment may refrain them from doing so. However, punishment does not incite individuals to give their best or to become champions in the field. Usually, rewards lead to more

DOI: 10.1057/9781137547378.0005

creative and innovative forms of cooperation than punishment. Any CEO of an innovative company is well aware of this; hence in start-ups, equity options are so popular. Indeed, rewards do make us work more effectively together while simultaneously strongly stimulate creativity, qualities punishments never will achieve. Be aware of extreme rewards that have become disentangled from the group as organization, allowing some top executives to disproportionally benefit from good group performance. MIT Finance professor Steward Myers therefore argues to adopt to a "new agency theory," in which there is nothing wrong with managerial "rents" (or rather high financial remuneration packages) as long as an efficient governance system avoids zero-sum games between managers and stockholders.[53] We could not agree less. However, the focus remains too tightly linked to the traditional agency theory where the concentration is on the principal/shareholder versus agent/manager relationship. In order to make the system of organizations competing for limited resources more sustainable, additional governance constraints of a more meaningful purpose is needed. A meaningful corporate objective that transcends the rat race for continuous more profits that almost deliberately harm particular critical stakeholders would be more sensible. Such a meaningful purpose allows leaders to incite cooperative behavior within the organization that transcends – or at least complements – the need to rely only on pecuniary reward and punishment.

In game theoretical language, one could claim that rather than withdrawing from cooperation – which could negatively affect the organization – one only withdraws from those who already has shown signs of defection, and one rewards those who do cooperate well and enable organizations to achieve their objectives. Interestingly enough, societies or communities where public cooperation is engrained and where people trust the police force and their law enforcement institutions – as in the Scandinavian countries – revenge is generally shunned. On the contrary, in countries like South Italy or Indonesia, where the rule of law is perceived to be ineffective, antisocial "revenge" punishments could easily erupt. Obviously, such institutional (legal) weaknesses lead to a suboptimal equilibrium that is inherently labile and unsustainable.

Maybe, the idea of what is good or bad, or what is even moral, may lay in the mechanism of reputation that seems to play an essential role in human societies. Many business tycoons have become very successful and wealthy because of building a reputation to be trustworthy, accountable, responsible and reliable. The venerable name that the Rothschild

DOI: 10.1057/9781137547378.0005

family has gained was the direct result of their impeccable behavior that they could be trusted, even under daring circumstances. In other words, the name of Rothschild and their subsequent business success and vast wealth creation is directly linked to indirect reciprocity. The opposite is also true. We all know of families (empires) who thrived for a while, but then were running out of "luck" because of the fact that some family members did not behave appropriately toward their business partners or clients – to say the least – with all the subsequent negative reputational consequences. *Give and you shall receive.* We all prefer to collaborate with individuals or organizations that have a good reputation and will avoid those with a negative reputation.[54]

Efficient groups need mechanisms that guarantee some loyalty from its members. Group cohesion favors an innate sense of group loyalty and a work ethics that entices individual members to adhere to the organizational values. As a matter of fact, any seasoned executive could have skipped those concepts out of Evolutionary or Game Theory by focusing on what drives operational effectiveness. Most would agree that a greater level of collaboration assumes to transcend organizational silos, and to share honest and transparent information across the organization.

How does one explain the success of Google, Apple, Facebook or Amazon in terms of network attraction? Their reputation! Since the number of links to a website closely relates to its reputational popularity, traffic and search-engine ranking, the most reputable will continue to dominate the web, as the "winner takes it all." Networks act like amplifiers and the World Wide Web can be perceived as a hub of highly connected individuals. The traditional hierarchical organizations, on the contrary, seem to become suppressors of creativity and innovation, as they ignore the principle of fluid network collaborations. In addition, certain structures of social network promote cooperative behavior better than other systems. Groups with a smaller number of people seem to function better to creatively collaborate than bigger groups with huge number of individuals because smaller groups usually are more efficient in performing specific tasks than big groups. We only need a few reputable friends on whom we can fully rely. An organization is not that different. Nonetheless, these relationships or networks are rather fluid since we are all subject to the ebb and flow of many influences. Indeed, we have a strong almost spiritual conviction that one reaps what one sows. Call it a "divine Tit-for-Tat."[55] Organizations are well aware that over a longer period one gets more from social living in a network of committed suppliers, loyal customers,

DOI: 10.1057/9781137547378.0005

engaged employees and a endorsing community than pursuing a solitary selfish maximization of mere profitability for the capital providers.

Collaboration and coordination between organizations is not new and we strongly believe that it will become much more prevailing out of necessity, not just because of enlightened attitude of the CEOs of those organizations. Tight inventory systems that limit working capital can cause phenomenal disruptions as the Fukuyama disaster has shown us. Similarly, in the automotive industry, in the spring of 2012, the factory of a major supplier of a chemical crucial in automotive fuel and braking systems blew up in Germany. With such tight inventory systems in the very competitive car manufacturers, much of the needed chemical was wiped out. Executives rightfully were worried about possible shortage of this chemical that could cause these manufacturers to being forced to stop their production lines. That would be an utter disaster in an industry with such tight margins. At a hastily convened meeting in Detroit, the big automakers and their suppliers gathered to explore new necessary options. They were able to expedite their parts-validation process enabling them to quickly replace the resin with alternatives.[56] Such a coordinated and well-executed joint plan paid off. But it also shows that when necessary – out of self-interest – cooperation (and not fierce competition) between organizations is possible.

Another example is in the health care industry where a unit of Novartis is closely collaborating with Google to develop contact lenses that can be used to monitor a person's health.[57] Such collaboration takes advantage of each other's expertise and core competencies to develop some new service or product to resolve or ease customer's challenges.

When Sunil Mittal, the owner of Bharti Airtel – the Indian tycoon who started from scratch to build the fourth largest global telecommunications company – decided to take on much bigger competitors, he decided to closely partner and collaborate with IBM and Nokia-Siemens-Network (NSN) to whom he outsourced the infrastructure of his new business model. He grew phenomenally, and through a USD 10.7 billion acquisition of the Zain group in Africa in 2010 that had a considerable mobile network business footprint in 15 African countries, he subsequently expanded his telecommunication group to more than 240 million subscribers in close allied partnership with his outsourcing partners IBM and NSN.[58] This "Indian Model" elevated the Bharti Airtel in the premier league through smart and cunning collaboration with international business partners, overcoming unnecessary wrangling

DOI: 10.1057/9781137547378.0005

about sharing profits by increasing the pie considerably to make such a cooperation worth it for all partners involved.

The whole progress in the internet and computer technology has been the direct result of in-group and (less obvious) between-groups collaboration at different levels. Bell Labs, Xerox PARC, HP, Intel, Microsoft, Google, Apple, Facebook, and even more explicitly WWW, the free open software such as Linux and Firefox, or the amalgam of numerous knowledge brought together for free into Wikipidia, and ultimately the Internet itself, would have never seen the daylight if it had not been for the incredible creative collaboration between a number of extraordinary inventors, entrepreneurs, idealists and investors. Business could be perceived as *collaboration* based on trust and outcome with the aim to *create a bigger pie* whereas *competition* focuses mainly on *dividing up* created value as in a zero-sum game.

Moreover, in this digital era, innovative collaboration between individuals, groups, universities, governments, among others – sometimes characterized by tensions and competition – is not just fuelled by the commercial desire to gain "benefit," but often driven by relentless passion to make a difference, to materialize a dream, to give meaning to the belief that one can change things.

Notes

1   Young 2015.
2   Rifkin 2014
3   Grant 2013.
4   Grant 2013: 9. The research indicates that givers, takers and matchers all can and do achieve success. But when givers succeed, it seems to spread and cascade, allowing a network to win, and not just the individual. From an evolutionary perspective, I would argue – based on Grant's point – that those givers are better placed to win more often in competition between organizations, because they can fall back on a trusted network that would back them up where necessary, whereas the takers and matchers have less social capital to spend.
5   Verhezen 2009; Granovetter 1983.
6   Grant 2013: 47.
7   Grant 2013. Indeed, according to networking experts, reconnecting in a wired world is a totally different experience for givers who have a track record of generously sharing their knowledge, helping other people. For takers, reactivating dormant ties is a real challenge because fellow takers

in the network may be suspicious or self-protective by withholding novel information. If the dormant ties are matchers, they will share only with other matchers or givers and may even punish takers as in the Ultimatum Game. And if, as Grant eloquently argues, a taker's self-serving actions were what caused a tie to become dormant in the first place, it may be almost impossible to revive the relationship at all.

8   Wilson 2015.
9   Dixit & Nalebuff 2010.
10 Frank 1988.
11 Charan 2015.
12 In order to remain fully transparent to the reader, it should be noted that Pri Notowidigdo is a friend, mentor and business partner of me in Indonesia. See his company's website: http://amrop.com/office/jakarta
13 Green 2013: 46–47. Gossiping also implies to make judgments and also that it comes naturally. Researchers have proven that babies at the age of six months, long before they can walk and talk, are able to make human judgments about actions and agents, "reaching out to individuals who show signs of being cooperative (caring about others) and passing over individuals who do the opposite." These judgments come naturally and are produced by automatic programs, sensitive to low-level cues, indicating that these moral judgments and the related gossiping are genetically inherited.
14 Quoted by professor Gazzinga 2011: 159. The social psychologist Nicholas Emler has studied the content of conversations and found that 80–90 percent are about specific names and known individuals, that is, social small talk.
15 For some introductory thoughts on Evolutionary Dynamics of Cooperation, see Nowak 2006b; Rand, Green & Nowak 2012.
16 Hardin 1968; Klein 2014; Nowak 2011. Many problems that challenge us today can be traced back to a profound tension between what is good for the selfish "short-term rational" individual and what is desirable for the good of society or community as a whole. That conflict can be found in global problems such as climate change, resource depletion, deforestation, pollution, overpopulation, poverty and even corruption. Nowak even goes so far to suggest that if we are to win the struggle for our existence, and "avoid a precipitous fall," there is no choice but to harness the creative force to cooperate across national political borders and organizational short term interests.
17 Dixit & Nalebuff 2010; Nowak 2006b. The PD is a theoretical game that captures the essence of cooperation in biological, social and business contexts. In the PD, cooperation – which is optimal for both players, but hardly reached in reality – is dominated by defection or selfish behavior at the expense of joint selfless behavior. The repeated PD is a tool for studying indirect reciprocity, which presents a mechanism for the evolution of cooperation. Tit-for-Tat (TfT) is a simple but successful strategy of indirect

reciprocity. TfT cooperates on the first move and then does whatever the opponent did in the previous round. Evolutionary analysis of "reactive strategies" reveals that TfT is a catalyst for the emergence of cooperation, but not the ultimate goal. The TfT is replaced by Generous TfT. However, both TfT and GTfT are outcompeted by Win-Stay, Lose-Shift (WSLS), which can correct the mistakes and is stable against neutral drift to all defects from cooperation. Both in evolutionary biology as well as in the real business world, there seems to be an ongoing oscillation of cooperative and defective societies or groups in a struggle of war and peace. These cycles are interrupted by the emergence of WSLS, which seems to dominate all generous cooperators and resist the invasion of all selfish defectors.

18   In that seminal paper of 1968, Hardin believes that only the intervention of a strong government – a third party – and governmental regulation could reduce this tragedy of commons as counterforce to the selfish interests of individual organizations that destruct the commons. If the public is misled in thinking that the risk for destructive climate change or gross pollution would be high, then they will be much more inclined to club together to curb climate change or pollution.

19   Rifkin 2014: 231. "A Common is that it is held in common and collectively managed." This new term of Commons in fact describes a newly evolving form of governance. Indeed, "the communication/energy/transportation matrices of the First and Second Industrial Revolutions required huge influxes of financial capital and relied on vertically integrated enterprises and centralized command and control mechanisms to capitalism, aided by government. The communication/energy matrix of the Third Industrial Revolution – the Internet of Things – is facilitated more by social capital than by market capital, scales laterally, and is organized in a distributed and collaborative fashion, making Commons management with government engagement the better governing model." It is expected that in the coming era, a tripartite partnership with Commons management will start an important role, complemented by government and private market forces.

20   Wilson 2015: 12; Ostrom 1990 & 2010. The late professor Ostrom identified eight core design principles required for "common pool resources" groups to effectively manage their affairs: (1) Strong group identity and understanding of purpose. The identity of the group, the boundaries of the shared resource, and the need to manage the resource must be clearly delineated. (2) Proportional equivalence between benefits and costs. Members of the group must negotiate a system that rewards members for their contributions. High status or other disproportionate benefits must be earned. Unfair inequality poisons collective efforts. (3) Collective-choice arrangements. People hate being told what to do but will work hard for group goals to which they have agreed. Decision making should be by consensus or another process that

group members recognize as fair. (4) Monitoring. A commons is inherently vulnerable to free-riding and active exploitation. Unless these undermining strategies can be detected at relatively low cost by norm-abiding members of the group, the tragedy of the commons will occur. (5) Graduated sanctions. Transgressions need not require heavy-handed punishment, at least initially. Often gossip or a gentle reminder is sufficient, but more severe forms of punishment must also be waiting in the wings for use when necessary. (6) Conflict resolution mechanisms. It must be possible to resolve conflicts quickly and in ways that group members perceive as fair. (7) Minimal recognition of rights to organize. Groups must have the authority to conduct their own affairs. Externally imposed rules are unlikely to be adapted to local circumstances and violate principle three. (8) For groups that are part of larger social systems, there must be appropriate coordination among relevant groups. Every sphere of activity has an optimal scale. Large-scale governance requires finding the optimal scale for each sphere of activity and appropriately coordinating the activities, a concept called *polycentric governance*.

21 Dixit & Nalebuff 2010; Nowak 2006a, 2006b. Such an suboptimal equilibrium in a PD has been mathematically proven by the late John Nash; hence the name: Nash optimum.

22 Nowak 2011: 269. According to mathematical biologist Nowak, cooperation arises out of competition, even though the two partners or individuals (or groups) are locked together in ceaseless conflict. "The collective effort of society depends in part on suppressing the ability of the individual to mutiny and defect. The same goes for rebellious cells, chromosomes, and genes. Like day and night, or good and bad, cooperation and competition are forever entwined in a tight embrace" (Nowak 2011: 10–11). Nowak claims that natural selection actually destroys what would be best for the entire population. Natural selection undermines the greater good, and favors only the best adapted individual or group. However, to favor cooperation, natural selection is "helped" by the mechanisms for the evolution of cooperation. Indeed, in reality, "evolution has used various mechanisms to overcome the limitations of natural selection. Over the millennia they have shaped genetic evolution, in cells or microbes or animals. Nature smiles on cooperation."

23 Dawkins 1989. This well-known Oxford sociobiologist has promulgated the Darwinian idea that animals – and human beings – possess an innate sense of fairness, at least for their kin and extended family members. Darwin has made similar claims that many animals have an innate "social instinct" that makes them seek companionship and even feel sympathy for other members of their species. Hence the inevitable conclusion that the Homo Sapiens has an innate sense of fairness and morality. It can be argued that sociobiology, based on William D. Hamilton's initial research, claims that altruism was really

DOI: 10.1057/9781137547378.0005

motivated by nothing but the egocentrism of our genes. And yes, individuals compete for resources within the group, but they cooperate and unite and work together against other groups to enhance their chances to survive.

24   Nowak 2006a: 76.

25   Klein 2014: 145–146. The intriguing and subtle notion of "The Right Amount of Generosity" eloquently summarizes the same findings in sociobiology as those found in Game Theory. "Thus altruism can only persist if altruists parcel out their service to others in the right dose. If they withhold too much, their sacrifice will not be effective and the community will be wiped out by other groups. But if they do too much good, they will fall behind vis-à-vis the takers in their groups. Over time, ruthlessness will win out, and in the long run, that community will also be destroyed." Therefore a right amount of generosity of cooperative behavior is required to optimize long-term survival.

26   Nowak 2011. If we assume that an organization is a living entity that aims to enhance its chances to survive and to "win" the competition, then it also can be assumed that organizations could learn something from living cells and organisms of beings, though with different characteristics. Similarly, every gene, every cell and every organism is designed to promote its own evolutionary success at the expense of its competitors, so it seems. Yet, genes and cells and even organisms cooperate to increase their survival chances.

27   Axelrod 1984; Nowak 2011; Nowak & Sigmund 1992. In the computer experiment organized by Axelrod, it was indeed the simple or neat Tit-for-Tat strategy by Rapoport that won the tournament several times. This can be described as a matcher strategy whereby you start out cooperating, and stay cooperative as long as your partner continues to cooperate with you. In case your counterpart chooses to defect to compete (with you), you will match that behavior by also switching from cooperation to competition. This was a highly effective game theoretical tournament winner. But the Tit-for-Tat suffers a fatal flaw, according to Harvard mathematical biologist professor Martin Nowak, of not purely copying the behavior and misinterpreting possible errors, which lead to destructive competitive behavior where all parties lose. Tit-for-Tat cannot correct mistakes, because an accidental defection usually leads to a long sequence of retaliation and revenge. Nowak's suggestion to be more generous – a Generous Tit-for-Tat or GTfT – and not immediately matching a possible error of immediately following the move and also switching from collaboration to competition. In other words, you still cooperate in response to one in three defections. A GTfT easily wipes out the TfT and is able to defend itself against being exploited by defectors. Nonetheless, GTfT carries a risk when takers rise up again and "surround" the generous givers to exploit them. However, in a world where reputations and relationships are becoming more visible, it is increasingly difficult

DOI: 10.1057/9781137547378.0005

for takers to take complete advantage of givers. And as long as there is a minimum cluster of 37 percent givers who are able to cooperate and benefit from this cooperation, the "nice people will win." The ultimate optimal solution, Nowak and Sigmund suggest, is the Win-Stay Lose-Shift strategy that has proven to be even more robust then either TfT and GTfT.

28 Such a suboptimal solution is a Nash equilibrium – as the Noble Prize winner John Nash, a mathematician, did discover that every strategic problem had at least one solution from which no player can deviate without the disadvantage to himself, although the solution may not be optimal.

29 All depends on how we define "altruism." If we would see "altruism" as "becoming part of something larger than oneself" then it may not necessarily result in unconditional other-centered behavior than could be easily exploited whereas in our definition, the other-centeredness is conditional since it requires a systemic approach to build something larger than ourselves allowing to become more adaptable to the environment in which we live (and thus it remains a relative rather than absolute notion), and thus increasing the chances to survive.

30 It is a term used by Nowak in his book *Supercooperators* (2011).

31 Grant 2013.

32 Nowak 2006a: 86–92. The Win-Stay, Lose-Shift (WSLS) strategy has the advantage over the winning TfT strategy that it can correct occasional mistakes, and it simply monitors its own payoff: "If I am doing well, I will continue with the present action; if I am not doing well, I will try something else." It is quite remarkable that this simple and fundamental and simple rule (of Win-Stay, Lose-Shift) easily outperforms both TfT and GTfT in the repeated PD. Nowak 2011: Cooperation with a good person (and I would say by extension with an organization) is regarded as good, while defection against a good person (or organization, I would argue) is regarded as bad. One seems to differentiate justifiable from nonjustifiable defection.

33 Nowak 2006a: 90.

34 Hansen, Ibarra & Peyer 2013.

35 Green 2013: 347. This philosopher elaborates how moral psychology can be useful in addressing some moral issues beyond our own tribal extended "kin and kith." He claims that cooperation at the highest level is

> inevitably strained, opposed by forces favoring Us over Them. [...] We've outsmarted most of our predators, from lions to bacteria. Today, our most formidable natural enemy is ourselves. Nearly all of our biggest problems are caused by, or at least preventable by, human choice. Recently, we have made enormous progress in reducing human enmity, replacing warfare with gentle commerce, autocracy with democracy, and superstition with science. [...] How can we do better? [...] universal features of human psychology allow Us to triumph over Me, putting us in the magic corner, averting the Tragedy of the Commons. [...] {But} Even when we think we're being fair, we unconsciously favor the version of fairness most congenial

DOI: 10.1057/9781137547378.0005

to Us. Thus, we face the Tragedy of Commonsense Morality: moral tribes can't agree on what's right or wrong.

36   Green 2013.

37   Interesting to note that from an organizational evolution perspective, group-level functional organization evolves primarily by natural selection between groups (Wilson 2015). That means that as long as group collaboration within this ecosystem is more "altruistic" than another cluster of group cooperation, that more collaborative functioning between a group of companies will evolve as the winners of the preferred growing ecosystem. Altruistic or collaborative behaviosr among companies evolves whenever between-group selection prevails over within-group selection, which means that when an environmental/ ecological disaster is about to strike, competition between groups may be eased to find a collaborative solution to ensure the survival of the group.

38   Rifkin 2014: 309. About 62 percent of GenXers and Millennials are attracted to the notion of sharing goals, services and experiences in "collaborative commons". These two generations differ significantly from the baby boomers and WWII generation in favoring access over ownership. Moreover, it seems that "collaborative consumption" is to become one the 10 ideas that may change the world.

39   The scientist Trivers was among the first in 1971 to establish the importance of repetitive encounters so that cooperation could emerge. Trivers seems to suggest that human emotions of gratitude, sympathy, guilt and trust and moral outrage grew out of the same sort of simple reciprocal Tit-for-Tat logic that governs biological life in general.

40   David Hume eloquently described this principle of direct reciprocity in his *A Treatise of Human Nature* (1740): "I learn to do service to another, without bearing him any real kindness; because I foresee, that he will return my service, in expectation of another of the same kind."

41   Nowak & Coackley 2013: 100–102.

42   Baier 1994.

43   Isaacson, 2014.

44   Nowak & Sigmund 1998.

45   Nowak 2013: 103.

46   Nowak 2011; Nowak 2013: 104. The chances that such a cooperative network cluster succeeds depends on whether the benefit-to-cost ratio of such cooperative network cluster is exceeding the average number of neighbors who may or may not collaborate. Moreover, forming a group that favors cooperation above free-riding or manipulation makes sense only when such a group benefits from that cooperation and thus is likely less to go extinct. Such an event is backed up by the fact that groups can easily punish free-riders or at least deter them with sanctioning for cheating on cooperation. Nonetheless, it is less clear – empirically speaking according to

Nowak – whether punishment of free-riders alone constitutes a mechanism that promotes collaboration within groups, favoring more cooperative individuals. Moreover, according to Nowak, the relative abundance of cooperators always seems to fluctuate around the mysterious and magic 31.78 percent. This means that "exploiters and exploited, cheats and the honest, abusers and abused can coexist, even without the guidance of a strategy" (2011: 79). In other words, clusters of cooperators can prevail, even if besieged by defectors.

47 Fehr & Gaechter 2002; Camerer & Fehr 2006.

48 One could easily argue that this form of indirect reciprocity is quite similarly associated with *the Golden Rule* – Do unto others as you would have them to unto you – since it binds an empathetic emotional feeling with the idea of indirect reciprocity: If I am good to another person today, somebody may be good to me in the future. Maybe, this powerful rule, which has deeply influenced how we humans think and how we have almost innately developed social and moral rules, seems to be at the heart of what it means to be human.

49 Ostrom 2010; Wilson 2015.

50 Fehr & Gaechter 2002; Fehr, 2015a. Altruism increases the volume of mutually beneficial economic exchanges because people are willing to keep obligations if there are enough people who behave altruistically, or who are willing to punish "altruistically" in case of free-riding. Such a sanctioning system, according to Fehr, in combination with the right norms and right education is able to generate altruistic cooperation and valuable public goods.

51 Verhezen 2010; Nowak 2011.

52 Rand, Dreber, Ellingsen, Fudenberg & Nowak 2009.

53 During his "doctor honoris cause" lecture at the University of Antwerp on 1 April 2015, professor Steward Myers argued for a more efficient corporate governance system avoiding zero-sum games but emphasizing that investors should be more concerned with rent-seeking managers who redistribute instead of create a bigger pie.

54 Bennedsen 2013, "East meets West. Rothschild's Investment in Indonesia's Bakrie Group", INSEAD Case. Nonetheless, the Jason Rothshild versus Bakrie saga reveals that a good reputation does not preclude family members from suffering USD 3 billion worth investment in a huge coal company in Indonesia but listed on the London Stock Exchange as a result of bad business decisions and or of being too greedy.

55 This notion of "divine" TfT has been quipped by Corina Tarnita who has collaborated with Michael Nowak; cf. Nowak 2011: 266.

56 Charan 2013: 78–80.

57 Charan 2015.

58 Charan 2013; Bose & Celly 2011.

DOI: 10.1057/9781137547378.0005

Part II

The Quest for Reputational Excellence

Verhezen, Peter. *The Vulnerability of Corporate Reputation: Leadership for Sustainable Long-Term Value.* Basingstoke: Palgrave Macmillan, 2015. DOI: 10.1057/9781137547378.0006.

▶

DOI: 10.1057/9781137547378.0006

Governing our digitized business context is mandatory for any corporation that acknowledges the crucial importance of reputation it can have on its financial bottom line. Governing the delicate challenge of maintaining or enhancing individual or corporate reputation[1] will require some wise decision making.

Most scholars and crisis managers emphasize the threatening risk component of reputation – losing trust and facing corporate crises. We believe that the intangible value of reputation – for instance, gaining the loyalty of customers and committed employees – is undervalued or not well understood, possibly because it is so hard to effectively measure reputational opportunities and threats.

What could boards do to improve reputational excellence? Approaching transparency, fairness, accountability and responsibility seriously – the main principles of good corporate governance – would be a good start. In addition, hoping for wise corporate leadership to unfold may also be necessary to address some of our global challenges. Reputational excellence would be a useful yardstick to incentivize such wise decision making.

Note

1   Macey 2013. Although we do not explicitly make the distinction, professor Macey convincingly argues that corporate reputation should be clearly distinguished from individual reputation. An individual's reputation at Wall Street, for instance, has gradually become unhinged from the reputation of the firm for which the person works. Macey analyses the assumptions of the old reputational school: (1) cheaters never prosper; (2) employees will always go down with the ship; and (3) corporate and individual reputations are joined into a single, unitary thing. All three of these assumptions have proven to be false when one analyzes the economic financial crisis at Wall Street and beyond. Only when individuals would act and be legally bound as partners in a partnership with personal legal liability to the partnership, there is some overlapping or convergence between the reputation of the individual and the corporation.

DOI: 10.1057/9781137547378.0006

3
Reputation in a Digitized World: Act Responsibly, Always

Abstract: *The digitization of our world has changed the way we do business. The digitization has drastically decreased the overall transaction costs between different parties, be it an opportunity for some or a threat for others. Some companies like Apple, Amazon, Airbnb have embedded this digitization into their core business model. But other more traditional companies are possibly following suit, embracing the benefit and productivity gains of information communication technology.*

However, social media are also exacerbating the risk to reputation for every company globally. Because of this increased transparency and pressure on companies to address key stakeholders' concerns using social media to get their message heard, board directors need to consider ways to include these demands while at the same time not jeopardizing their fiduciary duty to achieve the financial objectives.

Verhezen, Peter. *The Vulnerability of Corporate Reputation: Leadership for Sustainable Long-Term Value.* Basingstoke: Palgrave Macmillan, 2015.
DOI: 10.1057/9781137547378.0007.

DOI: 10.1057/9781137547378.0007

Our modern world looks more like an exchange network. Creating loyal (long-term) relationships based on trust seem to be latest adagio in corporate marketing. Does the digitization of our economy effect these relationships? How can big data mining[1] and big data analytics help us to change our relationships for the better? Is there a link between developing reputational excellence and corporate social responsibility? In an increasingly digitized business network, "acting responsibly, always" seems to be a reasonable and wise choice.

3.1   Reputational excellence in a digitized world

Our global economy is a complex network of exchange relationships in which trust enables information to flow between different people and groups more freely. Investing in social ties – social capital that is a synonym for *guanxi* or professional business networks – matters.[2] Groups and organizations with a reputation of safeguarding professional relationships and social ties can easily and more effectively increase productivity and create output through cooperation within groups and related organizations.

3.1.1   How digitization and social media can affect the firm's Reputation

In the information age, managers must assume that virtually everything they do will eventually come into the public domain. Transparency requirements are no longer a "nice option to have"; transparent behavior will be more and more imposed by those who have a real or perceived "stake" in the organization. Such stake is expressed through communication either in the form of gossip or in (online) media reports. In return, a company's reputation partially depends on an appealing *narrative that it creates through its actions and its communications.* How does an organization deal with criticism in the Social Media, especially when their corporate reputation is at stake, when their reputation has been severely criticized in the press, online or not? Experience and studies reveal that high-performing brands exhibit certain characteristics that allow them to easier track and improve their reputational positions in case of attack.[3] Successfully communicating the organization's stance in the potential crisis or media attack will be crucial.

DOI: 10.1057/9781137547378.0007

Conceptually speaking, news coverage – online or in print – is largely driven by (1) the interest of the audience and (2) the importance it carries for society. The consumer of news determines the audience interest, affecting the amount and likelihood of the coverage. Societal importance shapes the coverage, either describing the facts or adding commentary and advocacy. The potential for media advocacy and thus coverage is high when interest and importance are both high. In this segment, news is conveyed as a story, emotionally engaging, simplified and with heroes, villains and victims. Companies that happened to be featured in the social media have to carefully laver on this emotionally engaged reputational battlefield and need to avoid being characterized as the villain.

Firms will be more and more scrutinized by a number of stakeholders in terms of taking full responsibility for their activities throughout the supply chain, for instance. That includes safeguarding that the human rights of employees of Chinese or other Asian suppliers are respected, that minimum wages are paid and so forth. This interdependency causes reputation risks. And mass media may not only cover a story of irresponsible behavior, as in originating the news, but they may also amplify the facts by bringing the story into the living room. Great (reputation) damage can be inflicted on a firm when that happens. "Being right," or being on the right side of the law, does not ensure success. What matters is the public's *perception* of being right. That is why reputational risk transcends the legal structure of the company. A business can suffer because of the activities of another (supplier or allied partner). Companies are held accountable more and more for the business practices of suppliers or contractors.

That the "Internet word of mouth" can be very powerful to strengthen and often undermine the corporate reputation is a truth that does not need to be explained to DELL Computer. After the dot.com bubble debacle early 2000, DELL, like may others, was under pressure to cut its own costs to maintain market leadership. Subsequently, it outsourced a lot of its product support to India. Unfortunately, despite the promise of in-person service to consumers, the outsourcing policy backfired and resulted in a dramatic increase of US customers' complaints. Not long thereafter, in June 2004, the company experienced a crisis of reputation. It culminated with one disgruntled Internet-savvy customer in the United States - who had signed up for a service plan that guaranteed in-home service – blogging his complaints of DELL's broken promises on the Internet, causing a viral response on the Net. Within weeks, the

DOI: 10.1057/9781137547378.0007

"DELL Hell" blogs were taken over by the business media, Business Week and Fast Company, and then by the more traditional media outlets such as *Wall Street Journal, The Guardian* and *New York Times*. The media furore started to cause serious reputational damage.

DELL's initial response was based on a public relations approach geared to the mass media era, but flunked dramatically. It then changed course and improved its customer service by launching "Direct2Dell," and customer-oriented websites "Ideastorm" and "StudioDell" to allow any reaction to be channeled to DELL's own blogosphere, allowing some more direct control of the social media content. Around the same time this blog "Direct2Dell" was launched in June 2006, to add to the reputational damage, DELL experienced a flurry of negative media attention when one of its laptops ignited and burned at a conference in Japan. Nonetheless, it was decided to invest in reputation management, requiring DELL's management to understand the influence of new social media. In that context, the evolution of DELL's reputation in the blogosphere was tracked from 2005 to 2007 and analyzed in a rudimentary manner by distinguishing positive versus negative postings, trying to assess the sentiments of customers toward DELL.[4] This analytic tool combined up front qualitative analysis of posts with subsequent semantic word mining. It suggested that within the overall ecosystem of blogs talking about DELL, their own successful corporate blog represented only one (minimal) voice among many, discussing the company in the blogosphere. And despite all of DELL's investments to improve customer service since the initial reputational crisis in 2004–2005, the negative echo-effect of the initial "DELL Hell" blog persisted.[5] Moreover, it was magnified by a rapid growth in the blogosphere in that same period. It also meant that the blogosphere was becoming increasingly influential, generating a growing number of messages about every firm's reputation with the potential of having ever greater influence on customers.

Indeed, the growing prominence of the blogosphere and other web innovations is forcing companies to think about reputation management in a new manner. One of the key implications is that companies need to listen to the voice of their customers by monitoring the blogosphere, allowing those firms to swiftly identify concerns and issues, and act on the problems as quickly as possible before they start to reverberate through the internet in a less than flattering manner. In addition, firms need to communicate what and how they are reacting or proacting to particular

DOI: 10.1057/9781137547378.0007

challenges and issues.[6] The DELL case teaches us that the internet and social media can either destroy or enhance corporate reputation.

The web-enabled collective intelligence is a potential source of collaboration between the firm and the internet communities and customers to promote and strengthen their brand. For executives charged with managing the firm's reputation, they will need to listen more attentively to the multifaceted and sometimes cacophonous voice of customers in the blogosphere. Firms should not just be attentive to (potential) customers, but also listen to other potentially critical stakeholders who may affect the reputation of the firm. Nonetheless, organizations should distinguish mere noise from critical patterns or comments.

There is growing evidence that direct, strong, positive engagement between people is vital to promoting trustworthy, cooperative behavior. However, being connected through collaborative networks can be a double-edged sword. Recent research seems to suggest that collaborative in-house clustering could undermine performance by fostering an unproductive imbalance between the exploration of new ideas to resolve new challenges and the exploitation of ongoing operations. It is true that collaboration within groups significantly improves information gathering but it does not increase the likelihood of correct solutions because too much connectivity in organizational behavior can lead to premature and nonuseful consensus.[7] Just bringing together people and making them collaborate does not always guarantee better solutions.

Reputation is dependent not just on what is currently going on in the organization, but also what actions have been undertaken to prepare for the future. What shift is being prepared by leadership to guarantee some sustainability? Finding a balance between *exploiting* the *current* revenue stream resulting from present innovative products and services and *exploring future* potential new solutions through innovative collaboration within or between organizations is crucial for any management team. The visualization of such a life line in Figure 3.1 even assumes that leadership should continuously explore new commercially viable innovative products or services, and shift well before the declining stage, when it would be too late.

Exploration refers to how much the members of a group bring in as new ideas from outside, which in turn predicts both innovation and creative output. These new business ideas could be related to new products or reducing waste as found in "frugal innovation," doing more with

DOI: 10.1057/9781137547378.0007

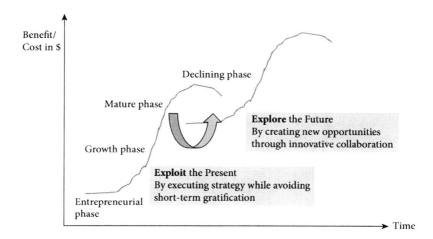

FIGURE 3.1   *A life line of an average organization: exploitation and exploration*
Source: Design by Verhezen 2015.

less input. Such kind of innovation embraces the understanding that sustainability needs to be part of our strategies.

If we assume that innovation is among the most important drivers of long-term performance, managers should be encouraged to explore for new ideas by helping employees establish diverse connections between people, in other words, by helping groups of employees to collaborate across border. At the same time, exploration outside the group should avoid some biasedness of "groupthink."[8] Paradoxically, to survive systemic risks, one needs not just one "best" cooperative system but rather a varied set of diverse and even competing systems in which groups of individuals intensively collaborate with each other.[9] According to MIT expert Pentland, decisions do not happen in a vacuum and often draw on the experiences of others. Diversity and independency definitely help innovative ideas. The success of good and wise decisions greatly depends on the quality of social exploration and diverse group collaboration while avoiding the echo chamber, the biasedness and herd behavior of groupthink.[10]

In our Digitized World, the amended "wisdom of the crowd" resides in between the extremes of isolation and the herd behavior of the biasedness of groupthink. Nowadays, commercially viable "inventions" and innovative products are usually the result of teamwork although some individuals are more creative and more exhibit more "expertise" than others. Too tight social groups often experience "echo chambers" where everyone does the same, since their members tend to share information, or when there may be heavy social pressure to hold the same opinions. Social networks almost function like a fractal dance of learning that spins ideas into useful innovative products and services.

The Australian ICT entrepreneur Warren Weeks,[11] has developed a quite advanced analytical algorithm tool combined with smart heuristics through his firm, Cubit Media Research, to enable organizations to analyze big online data more effectively to seek reputational excellence and to minimize reputation risks. Cubit's research revealed the presence of eight success indicators in the communications profiles of brands that stand out in terms of market share, stock market performance and customer satisfaction as found in attitudinal surveys.[12]

Optimizing a firm's reputation is possible only when it is first of all able to maintain an *experiential ecosystem,*[13] delivering experiences to customers and stakeholders. Apple or Harley Davidson are examples of such "love(d) brands" that offer experiential ecosystems surrounding and beyond their products. These experiences make them extremely credible or "reputable," but simultaneously also make them extremely vulnerable to potential violations of those expected experiences.

Second, any such firm needs to analyze its *emotional profile* in the social media and react where appropriate. Poor labor practices at the Taiwanese Foxconn company in Shenzhen, China – leading to worker suicides – had been widely discussed on China's Sina Weibo and other social media worldwide. It forced Foxconn's largest client, Apple, to belatedly take public action. Indeed, by publicly and personally apologizing, Apple's CEO Cook addressed the alleged ethical violations in Foxconn. And the fact that the highest executive made time to transparently address the ethical misbehavior of a major supplier helped Apple to regain some of its credibility in this highly sensitive ethical issue. However, had Apple been more swift to address the social media frenzy about these suicides at Foxconn, the firm could have avoided some reputation damage. Apple could even have built up some reserve of goodwill to counter any future attacks for other corporate social responsibility. Indeed, a clear, succinct and consistent message by the firm is needed to counter possible media onslaught on the firm's reputation.

Furthermore, companies can use a "message-driven differentiation" that tracks the extent to which an organization is able to cater to the different stakeholders' interests, be it financial performance, corporate strategy, the delivery of promised products and services' quality, or

DOI: 10.1057/9781137547378.0007

the community and environmental impact. Such message profiling is a useful way of assessing how organizations are succeeding (or not) to communicating their strengths in specific areas of interest to a range of stakeholder groups. Remarkable is that only a few companies focus on environment and community. Most of the attention is paid to the products, their finance and the corporate strategy, as one could expect with public listed companies that seem to comply with the expectations from investors to quarterly meet or exceed the financial expectations. With the digital online media, stakeholders can become more influential; they can hurt the reputation of the firm if not well handled.

A *Messaging Mix Dimension* analyzes how companies and brands utilize a broad spectrum of techniques to capture the audience focus, whereas a *Media Channel Mix* rates the organization's relative success in utilizing a range of media channels in their communication efforts, tended to engage diverse audiences with a variety of traditional and nontraditional channels, matched to the tone of each channel. Research by Cubit Media Research in 2012–2013 has shown that the National Australian Bank, for instance, is using its twitter presence more effectively than its competitors ANZ and Commonwealth Bank to cater to certain audiences. However, Commonwealth Bank then is superbly promoting its online and mobile services, essential to customer satisfaction within the banking sector, increasing its reputation among existing and potential customers.[14]

Finally, an analysis on the "broad-spectrum modality" and *halo effect* can sway some stakeholders to re-view the perception about a company. For instance, Samsung's lack of less formal local social media engagement, coupled with a tendency toward the use of a more reserved tone in the traditional media, and not even any positive "halo effect" of a recognizable top executive, meant it underperformed in terms of brand communication in the Australian market.[15]

Experts will tell firms to stop thinking that everything is just like it used to be, and to recognize that communication is not just about advertising but involves investment in good integrated monitoring and communication analysis tools.[16] Traditional and social media reports have a huge impact on organizational prosperity – because they shape corporate reputation. The death of a young female driver of a Volkswagen in Melbourne in 2012, allegedly due to a mechanical problem, had huge negative impact on the revenues of the company in Australia in the subsequent two years.[17] Messages are not just about the facts; it's almost always about the *context*, the level of *engagement* and the *emotive*

DOI: 10.1057/9781137547378.0007

representation around an issue that has the most (negative) impact on the firm's reputation. Hence firms need new tools and new thinking in order to win in this new media environment – and to stay focused on their reputations. That will require top executives and the board to drive changes that address the reputation risk and to possibly attempt to move to the sweet spot of reputational excellence.

3.1.2   Good reputation resulting from "good profits"

Partners in consulting or legal firms – who often collaborate with others – are well aware that referrals are a much more efficient way to generate revenues than prospecting on their own. Referrals are based on built reputation as a team player. Reputation of being a team player helps to substantially increase the referral rate. The compounded effect of word of mouth is powerful, as colleague-experts may recommend us to others. Because of these recommendations and referrals, our reputation is likely to grow significantly over time. And with this improved reputation, built on established trust to be able to work with peers more quickly and with less tension, fruits can be harvested. Indeed, significant financial benefits from such a reputation build up over the years.[18] In other words, specialized advisory services firms understand that by serving the most complex needs of some of their clients, they will earn their loyalty and a considerable market share of the most valuable revenue streams. That same "glowing" effect of having a good reputation among partners and best employees-experts can be as influential for loyal customers.

eBay's lofty and high-minded principles on their website,[19] for example, did not remain empty words as often found in recruitment brochures, but have been translated into daily priorities and decisions. The majority of eBay's customers are satisfied and often are very loyal followers. Consequently, referrals generate more than half of the site's new customers, creating multiple economic advantages. It seems that eBay – like other trusted brands such as Amazon – relies more on word of mouth than on advertising and traditional marketing, giving them a substantial competitive advantage. Moreover, eBay has learnt to tap the creativity of an entire online community, encouraging everyone to criticize and provide feedback in order to improve their services to the customer and online community. And it should be emphasized that eBay's structure and processes enable each member using eBay to establish a reputation based not on public relations but on the cumulative experience of members with whom they have established a business relationship.

DOI: 10.1057/9781137547378.0007

Deep respect for the power of word of mouth is based on the simple but fundamental *Golden Rule* "Do unto others what you like to be done to you." This rule seems to become engrained in our (un)consciousness: when we treat people right, the way we ourselves would want to be treated, it makes us feel good, creating energy and motivation in the process. Indeed, eBay's founder Pierre Omidyar refers to his mother who taught him that Golden Rule to have a deep respect for other people, which he subsequently made the corner stone value of his successful company. Other corporate leaders such as the CEOs of Southwest Airlines and the Four Seasons – both excelling in great employee treatment that subsequently is translated into above-industry-average customer service – also invoke that same Golden Rule to install certain values into the organizational culture. And it is this created loyalty that is the key to "better" profitable growth.

Sustainable "better" growth is possible only when good profits are distinguished from bad profits. Bad profits are about extracting value from customers instead of creating value.[20] When firms extract instead of create value for customers, we can speak of *negative reciprocity*. Managers, in an effort to push up short-term "bad" profits to enhance their own welfare with respect to bonus remuneration, may reduce the value offered to customers either through unjustified price increases or reduction in the quality of their products and services. They are, in essence, transferring value from customers to the firm, and ultimately to themselves through bonuses. In that case, managers not only reduce value for their customers, they also may destroy shareholder value over time by eroding goodwill. When a corporation focuses on creating shareholder value – even when that would imply to extract value from customers – it will likely create dissatisfied customers who may become *detractors*. The damage for such a corporation can be dramatic since those detractors are customers who not just cut back on their purchases, but may switch to the competition if they can and may even warn others to stay away from the company. Those detractors can easily tarnish the firm's reputation, diminishing its ability to recruit or retain the best employees and customers. Even if boards and senior management focuses on creating shareholders' value, a possible addiction to bad profits can demotivate employees and other critical stakeholders. Despite some possible very short-term windfalls, shareholders should be wary about such "bad" profits since the resentment by other stakeholders may undermine the company's prospects in the future. Such bad profits should be avoided.

DOI: 10.1057/9781137547378.0007

"Good" profits, however, function quite differently: a company earns good profits when it is able to offer real solutions to its customers, possibly creating some loyalty in the process. These customers are not only willingly coming back for more purchases, they also *promote* and recommend the company to friends and family. These referrals constitute the "goodness" of the profits generated. And we can easily assume that the best-known and reputable companies have generated a high degree of loyalty among their customers and employees, and likely among their investors as well, be it Vanguard in the mutual funds industry, Amazon. com in the online business or Southwest Airlines in the budget airline segment or Singapore Airlines in the premium-class airline segment. All of those companies can count on loyal customers and proud employees who carry the firm, resulting in impressive sustainable or consistent profit levels.

If the distinction between "bad" and "good" profits clearly shows differences in long-term profitability, why then most companies are not following the good advice by embracing the "Golden Rule"? Accounting procedures do not necessarily distinguish "good" from "bad" profit. And financial accounting revenues and margins – not necessary real economic profitability – determine how managers fare in their performance reviews. The importance of these customer promoters is overlooked because they do not show up on anybody's profit and loss statement or balance sheet. So the pursuit of (bad and occasionally good) profit dominates corporate and management agendas, while accountability and responsibility for building and preserving good relationships with customers and other critically relevant stakeholders gets lost in the shadows of accounting figures.

On the basis of these insights, Fred Reichheld and his colleagues at Bain & Company created a feedback system to connect loyalty and growth, which resulted in the infamous *Net Promoter Score* (NPS) System.[21] Asking that simple and "ultimate" question "how likely is it that you would recommend this company to a friend or a colleague" resulted in the Net Promoter Score system.[22] In a way, the NPS is fine-tuning traditional reputation measurements by explaining how building relationships worthy of loyalty translated into superior profits and growth. Those companies with the most efficient growth engines operate at NPS efficiency ratings of 50–80 percent. But the average firm splutters along at an NPS efficiency of only 5–10 percent where promoters barely outnumber detractors. Many firms and industries have negative NPS,

DOI: 10.1057/9781137547378.0007

which means that they continuously create more detractors than promoters by discouraging their customers.[23] However, the Net Promoter Score does help companies to identify customers who help their business and those who harm it. Through social media, customers can easily express that loyalty or anger on the internet. By quantifying the value of promoters or detractors in comparison with average customers, managers are in the position to evaluate investments aimed at improving the customers' experience and thus their loyalty. Investing in their loyal core clientele, addressing the concerns and issues of detractors and finding additional promoters that will help to generate referrals will create valuable goodwill or corporate reputation.[24] Through this process of NPS feedback, the company can significantly reduce the reputation risk and can excel its customer service, thereby enhancing its corporate reputation. Building good customer relationships boots a company's growth potential into adjacent service areas as the successful ecosystem of Amazon.com convincingly proves. What makes NPS an interesting predictive metric is the ability to answer the *why* behind building good relationships and to retain customers.

Many companies do not even realize how addicted they are to bad profits: Bain & Co has estimated that for the average firm, more than two-thirds of customers are bored passives or angry detractors.[25] That would mean that most attempts to invest or buy growth simply burn up shareholder capital. Inflated customer satisfaction scores have lulled these companies into complacency. And instead of creating consistent shareholder value over a longer period, investment to initiate or sustain growth rates are likely not well guided, to say the least. Every transaction consists of two components, a substance and a shadow. The substance is easily measured by the accounting system indicating where and how money changes hands. The shadow, however, takes place in the customer's heart and mind and revolves around a question for future behavior. It is this *shadow of the future*, expressed in reputation, that will indicate whether or not a currently successful company will be able to keep "sustainably" growing. *Exploiting the substance* is necessary, but the *exploration of this shadow (of the future)* may be even more important for the survival of the company over a longer period.

Similarly, Kim and Mauborgne's latest research on *Blue Ocean Leadership* indicates that only a small percentage of employees are really engaged in and committed to their work.[26] Hardly 30 percent of the total labor force has been perceived as sincerely fully committed and engaged, with

DOI: 10.1057/9781137547378.0007

50 percent bored and passive and 20 percent actively disengaged employees. This huge portion of uncommitted and disengaged employees can seriously undermine the potential productivity of companies.[27] What could be the reason for this widespread employee disengagement? Poor leadership is once more a key cause. Most executives acknowledge that one of their biggest challenges is closing the vast gap between the potential and the realized talent and the energy of the people they lead. Good leadership knows how to turn around such a situation.[28] Blue Ocean Leadership achieves a transformation toward more engaged and committed employees with less time and effort, because leaders are not trying to alter employees' personality, but tap into their potential to get to the core of leadership, inspiring and leading subordinates in an effective and efficient manner by valuing relationships among others. Such transformation not only positively affects the reputation of the leaders but also the corporate reputation of the firm to provide more meaning in the labor place.

What if we extend this notion to measure the value of relationships and their subsequent reputation to other critical stakeholders? Results may even look much darker! Nonetheless, committed leadership should attempt to benefit from increasing the symbolic capital of reputation into better and expanded social capital of good relationships. Symbolic and social capital can then rather easily be turned into economic capital and good profitability. And if the Golden Rule can be translated into promoter customers, one may also be able to apply that same rule to long-term investors, committed employees and a community that endorses a responsible corporation.

3.2 Corporate responsibility and its "glowing effect" on corporate reputation

Information that might once have been safely owned and being proprietary by management and boards can now escape the confines of the corporate borders and gain viral public exposure. Another consequence is that the traditional agency costs between management on the one hand and shareholders and boards on the other hand may have shifted, and consequently may have slightly changed the power structure between boards and top management. Let us focus on the power of information on the internet and its effect on the accountability and responsibility of top management and corporate boards.

DOI: 10.1057/9781137547378.0007

3.2.1   Increased scrutiny of accountability and responsibility

These days everyone has almost immediate access on their electronic devices to digital information and anyone who believes to have a stake in the organization can formulate and express an opinion, usually a superficial expression and not necessarily scientific. Social media are exacerbating the risk to reputation for every company globally. Moreover, the digitization has drastically decreased the overall transaction costs between different parties, be it an opportunity for some or a threat for others. Some companies like Apple, Amazon, Facebook, Airbnb, eBay and many other Internet-companies have embedded this digitization into their core business model. But other more traditional companies are possibly following suit, embracing the benefit and productivity gains of information communication technology. The more brick and mortar companies like Kaiser Permanente (KP), a Californian-based health insurance company that also runs clinics and community hospitals, invested a staggering USD 4 billion to automate and digitize all its processes.[29] In doing so, it created a distinctive competitive advantage resulting in superior performance in health care. Its speedier treatment reduced death from infection with more than half, making KP hospitals the most effective in terms of infection deaths in the United States. Now, interestingly, KP consciously decided to share its finding and methods with other players in the health care field. This form of altruistic cooperation and the grand results from data access and process improvement significantly boosted KP's corporate reputation, not only within its industry, but also far beyond. Because of its clear purpose – delivering care for a living – the CEO of KP collaborated with the federal government to improve nationwide policies. This is a clear example of leadership taking a stance, and despite the unpredictable world, carving a path in this uncertainty to create a "new" and profitable world of health care.

Some committed stakeholders, such as customers or NGOs, may launch claims that corporations can no longer ignore. Focusing on explicit and easy-to-specify contractual claims of investors or bondholders is a fiduciary duty and legal necessity. But ignoring the implicit claims of noninvestor stakeholders such as the promise of continuing service or product quality to customers or not harming the socioecological environment may be risky. Nonetheless, the market may be too fickle in the short term to use "corporate shared value" as sole criteria to determine corporate success, though it may become more reliable over a longer time period.

DOI: 10.1057/9781137547378.0007

The belief that business must serve multiple constituents has given way to an imperative to prioritize the shareholder. "The social responsibility of business is to increase its profits" as Milton Friedman eloquently but too narrowly expressed more than four decades ago. Every seasoned executive and board member knows, however, that value creation is viable only when an organization is sufficiently trusted by its stakeholders, be it committed employees or loyal customers. Maybe not just the owner and capital providers need to be rewarded for their investment, but also those committed stakeholders who have invested their time (as employees do), or have vested their trust in the company (as customers, suppliers and the community at large do).

We have seen examples of how customers can ruin the reputation of a firm through the blogosphere, but in the same vein, companies like Harley Davidson have greatly benefited from the loyalty expressed by their customers. The HOGs (Harley Owners' Group) are known all over the world and aspire more admiration today than fear as it was in the old days. However, not just customers or employees use the blogosphere to make their perspective and perception known to the (internet) community; anyone can express his/her opinion on the internet. Activist shareowners with an insignificant equity stake in the firm, for instance, can nowadays affect the firm by stirring up rebellion at negligible cost, independent of whether it is owned by families or widely held. And by the same token, corporations can creatively use social media to improve stakeholder loyalty and improve performance. Because of this increased transparency and pressure on the company to address particular stakeholders' concerns, board directors need to educate themselves about the technology, terminology and content of the use of social media. Board members cannot afford anymore to ignore these stakeholders who are using the social media to get their perception heard.

The traditional Chinese proverb, "doing good and not wanting others to know it," is not very suitable anymore in an ever mediatized corporate world. Communicating your objectives and purposes – and thus related activities to achieve those – is primordial in the era of social media and increasing scrutiny of corporate activities. It may even require a kind of paradigm shift.

3.2.2   Enhancing corporate reputation through "CSR" and "ESG" activities

There is a growing pressure on businesses to do more to solve social and environmental problems. Some leading companies are taking on the challenge of sustainability, not only to reduce their environmental foot-print bolstering their corporate reputation, but also to improve operational efficiency. Corporate social responsibility (CSR) should not just be bolting morality onto some marketing actions, but building responsible behavior into the strategy of the organization. Indeed, CSR could be considered as a form of strategic investment, creating reputation on the upside and preserving reputation on the downside. Companies like the Brazilian cosmetics firm Natura or the shoe manufacturer Puma have engrained corporate responsibility into their strategy. By embracing ESG and CSR, their corporate reputation has been considerably enhanced. This "people, planet, profit" engagement, in fact, indicates what those organizations are standing for. Another remarkable story is the historical turn-around of the Belgian industrial company Umicore from a traditional mining and exploration company to a world-class player in recycling and reusing high-tech materials and minerals that are used in a variety of products as in cars' exhaust filters, for example. "Minerals for a better life"[30] has become Umicore's purpose, turning the company into a highly perform-ing and inspiring organization that is both accountable for its financial performance to its shareholders as it is responsible for its various activi-ties that have a positive impact on their broader environment.

Besides the ecological soundness of an organization's activity, their CEOs and management are also expected to behave ethically and take social responsibility seriously, be it respect for human rights, fighting corruption, or human development, in the different places and commu-nities in which they operate. Quite a number of companies have invested in ethics training and compliance programs, but unethical behavior in business nevertheless persists. That is because managers are blinded to unethical behavior by cognitive biases and organizational systems.[31] Some of those biases may derail even the best intentioned managers: goals that reward unethical behavior; conflicts of interest that motivate people to ignore bad behavior; a tendency to overlook dirty work that has been outsourced to third parties; and inability to notice when behavior dete-riorates very gradually; and a tendency to overlook bad behavior when the outcome benefits the organization.[32] Management and top leadership should be aware of these biases and distorted incentive systems and care-fully remove hurdles that inhibit ethical behavior, as the global financial crisis has shown.

Executives are coming under a new pressure to become more transparent. Customers, investors and employees are becoming better

DOI: 10.1057/9781137547378.0007

informed about what businesses do around the world as a result of the information technology evolution. Consequently, they can exert global influence to change corporate behavior. The car manufacturer Kia, for instance, has drastically improved its product quality and reliability and statistically estimated its product failures. Kia's corporate reputation has become a competitive weapon. By making a credible, binding and costly promise to customers in the form of a warranty of seven years for their cars some years ago, Kia sent a strong message to the industry by linking this strategic bet to its corporate reputation. A "gamble" that is apparently paying off in Europe and the United States where Kia – now as part of the Hyundai group – has dramatically increased market share at the expense of other manufacturers.

Some other prominent businesses like the American retailer Costco or food distributor Wholefood,[33] the Danish pharmaceutical multinational Novo Nordisk, or the British-Dutch food conglomerate Unilever appear to take a serious stand on addressing broader social and environmental issues. Traditional corporations are even "purchasing" the reputation of collaborative "disrupters." For instance, instead of trying to use its existing business to compete with car-sharing services, Avis acquired Zipcar in 2013. Other examples of corporations-buy-into-CSR-reputable-companies are Unilever purchasing the venerable Ben & Jerry brand or Danone acquiring Tonyfield Farm. One can only hope that these multinational companies now take sustainability and social agendas more seriously, learning from their acquired smaller companies. Nonetheless, to continue to be a premium-priced brand known for its blended value approach[34] while being part of a multinational company remains challenging.[35]

It can be agreed that *corporate social responsibility associations* are related to the reputational status of a company as a good member of society with regard to social, environmental, ethical or even political issues. Ben & Jerry's ice cream, now part of Unilever, has been known for its dedication to social communities and environmental causes. Such CSR associations need to be distinguished from *corporate ability associations* that are related to a company's ability and professional expertise to produce high-quality products and services such as IBM or Apple, for instance. Interestingly, when a reputational crisis hits a corporation, it seems that having positive CSR associations are more beneficial to the company than having positive prior corporate ability associations.[36] The previously described Mercedes A-Model "Mooz" test debacle confirms

DOI: 10.1057/9781137547378.0007

this conjecture. In other words, corporates need to present themselves as good corporate citizens, both in normal business situations as in crises.

Being a good corporate citizen can be expressed through sustainability or programs where environmental, social and governance (ESG) concerns are properly dealt with in a strategic manner. There is not always necessarily a trade-off between financial and nonfinancial objectives. In order to achieve the desired enlightened objectives, companies need to think through which ESG issues are crucial and "material" for the company. Subsequently, by quantifying the improvements of these ESG issues one could measure the financial impact.[37] And communicating how the corporation is improving its ESG with stakeholders possibly secures a two-way dialogue. Obviously, taking ESG and CSR seriously will demand change. And to facilitate such change process, companies must break down certain barriers such as incentive systems and investor pressure that only emphasize short-term profitability, a shortage of required new expertise in ESG matters and capital-budgeting limitations that do not account for projects' environmental and social value.

Corporate social responsibility activities have become more mainstream. Companies approach environmental issues now with profit margins in mind. Recent research indicates that organizations can benefit from an appealing purpose as well as from investing in *frugal innovation* based on sustainability.[38] Indeed, by taking environmental measures in anticipation of future regulatory requirements, organizations *forestall risks*. Coca-Cola, for instance, plans to achieve "water neutrality" by 2020 – meaning that Coca-Cola will replenish all the water it uses in beverage production. Second, by investing in sustainability, organizations can considerably increase their *operational efficiency* by saving energy or reducing waste. IBM, for example, reduced its electricity consumption by 6.4 billion kilowatt hours between 1990 and 2013, saving USD 513 million. WalMart reports to have saved more than USD 200 million annually through its waste reduction efforts. Third, although the majority of consumers are not yet willing to pay a premium for green products, the niche of green shoppers is rapidly increasing into a powerful *environmental niche*. A funky company like method,[39] a cleaning-products supplier founded in 2000, offers products that are 100 percent natural, totally biodegradable. The company aims to provide best-smelling green soap that "cleans like heck and smells like heaven," based on the concept of *frugal innovation* (do more with less): its products include a plant-based laundry detergent that is eight times the normal concentration and thus is able to do more with less.[40] The eco-sustainable company disrupted the staid world of cleaning products and was acquired by Ecover in 2012 to form the world's largest green cleaning-products supplier. Another interesting example is Whole Foods: their annual revenues have increased steadily in the past five years, due to environmentally friendly products, according to a study by the Boston Consulting Group. And there is the booming "sharing economy" (where products and services are shared rather than owned) that are built around monetizing shared resources, thus cutting down on carbon consumption and other environmental costs. Uber's, Zipcar's and Airbnb's success can be explained by this growing trend, whereby the corporate reputation plays a crucial role to capture a growing number of customers, trusting the brand to do the right thing. That the business model of Airbnb, for instance, requests the customer to pay only 24 hours after having seen and experienced the room has created an insurmountable competitive advantage. More recently, firms and consumers have started to reduce, recycle and reuse products, giving rise to a "circular economy" (the indefinite reuse and recycling of materials). Adopting sustainable business practices to boost performance applied only by one in ten companies– could save the global consumer-goods sector alone USD 700 billion annually.[41] Patagonia, the outdoors company in California – has gained enormous attraction and reputation by promoting the reuse and recycling of their products by reselling them as secondhand. Another example is the multinational tile company Tarkett that equips homes, offices, hospitals and stores with tiles and flooring. Tarkett has always seen itself as a good corporate citizen that respected the wider society. The eco-friendly company has become the industry benchmark for achieving high standards in sustainability and has become a "circular economy" company.[42] The company is not only outstanding in terms of sustainability but has provided shareholders with a continuous reasonable return of investment.

Firms that tend to make their stakeholders – especially customers – better off will be the ones that are able to retain their loyal support. Value creation is nothing else than the sum of the utility created for each of the organization's legitimate stakeholders:[43] call it "Triple Bottom Line" thinking or "Corporate Responsibility." More and more executives acknowledge that this multiple-perspective or stakeholder approach at least complements if not supplements the prevailing shareholder value theory.

DOI: 10.1057/9781137547378.0007

Notes

1 Professor Pentland (2014) calls this *Social Physics,* which uses "socioscopes" to analyze and to understand social phenomena that are made up of billions of small transactions between individuals – people trading not only goods and money but also information, ideas or gossip. Big data give us the chance to understand, to analyze a society in all its complexity through the millions of networks of person-to-person exchanges.

2 Verhezen 2009; Putnam 2000.

3 Dowling & Weeks 2008; Weeks 2014.

4 Del Vecchio, Laubacher, Ndou & Passiante 2011.

5 Del Vecchio et al. 2011: 141–142. The reaction of DELL to launch its own blog was partially successful. The blog provides a platform for convening a community of prospective customers in a setting where its brand was prominently represented, while at the same time open and honest exchange of opinions generated useful feedback for the company.

6 Del Vecchio et al. 2011: 142. The researcher highlights the importance of communication since "action without engagement can lead to a situation in which a company's bad reputation outlasts positive changes to its service delivery; and engagement without action can lead to cynicism."

7 Berstein, Shore & Lazer 2015 in Organizational Science, quoted in Nobel, HBS Working Knowledge, 4 May 2015: Research & Ideas.

8 Pentland 2008, 2013 & 2014. Some researchers as Pentland from MIT even claim that network intelligence provides an extremely strong clue to better decision making in groups and organizations, optimizing rewards while avoiding expensive mistakes. Objective data from social network structures proved to be twice as accurate as even the best individual estimates and five times better than simple averaging of people's bets. Moreover, Pentland's research (2013: 68) shows that managers of teams with high levels of commitment, engagement and trust become more integrated into the team and will operate more democratically, resulting in much better performance compared to other less integrated teams. Pentland has labeled this network intelligence system as "social physics" because it provides a new, practical method that specifies how to create social incentives that establish more cooperative behaviors, and so improve everyone's situation. "Social physics gives us new cost-benefit equations that work better than economic incentives and opens up new practical opportunities to promote cooperation" (2014: 75).

9 Pentland 2014: 210–212. "All of this suggests that in order to maintain the robustness of the entire society, we need a diverse set of competing social systems, each with its own way of doing things, together with fast methods of spreading them when required. This sort of robustness is exactly what we achieve when we tune a system for the best flow."

DOI: 10.1057/9781137547378.0007

10   Pentland 2013: 86. Indeed, the search for new ideas and information, like the formation of new habits, appears driven primarily by social pressure, while some innovative champions may be an inspiring source for new ideas. Within this process of oscillation between *exploration* of new ideas by inventive creative individuals and *engagement* within group collaboration appears to increase the creative output by building up a more diverse store of experiences.

11   Warren Weeks was introduced to me as a mentor of a student of mine at the University of Melbourne. Ever since we met in 2010, we have continued to meet each other to share and discuss ideas and thoughts around governance and reputation, and how social media has significantly affected the management of corporate reputation.

12   Weeks 2014. Cubit's Dimension-8 framework analyzes the following critical success factors:

> (1) Experiential Ecosystem focus: understanding that these days, it is about more than just the product or services; (2) Profile: generating a comparative "critical mass" of volume and consistency of media attention; (3) Broad-based Regard: the favorability of commentary surrounding all the various aspects of a brand in line with a Reputation Narrative; (4) Messaging: clarity, concentration and consistency; (5) IEMFC: crafting communiqués that match the various stages of a buying cycle, i.e. interest, educate, motivate, facilitate, and cultivate behavior; (6) Media Mix: recognizing that different audiences will prefer different channels and will respond best when addressed through their channel of choice; (7) Broad-spectrum Modality: the ability to use the right communication mode to connect with key communities-of-interest in a balanced effort; and (8) the Halo effect: where it is present, thus typically comes from a strong personality associated with the organization, some historical aspect of the brand, or some uniqueness that sets it apart. Few brands carry a genuine halo effect – either positive or negative. But when they do, it can be a powerful influencer: think of Apple or Rolls Royce versus Enron.

13   Weeks 2014: Experiential Eco-System refers to the ability of some organizations to create fresh aspects of the product or service, that is, the value proposition offering, beyond just the products or services they sell. For Lexus, it is membership to the Lexus club that comes with the purchase of one of its cars, similar to the HOGs, the venerable and famous Harley Davidson's Owner's Group.

14   Weeks 2014.

15   Weeks 2014.

16   Weeks 2015. In order to establish a good communication and crisis management, firms need to eliminate the filter effect, which implies that top executives and boards should receive direct and not filtered information to take sensible and reasonable decisions. Moreover, only top executives and boards can drive a change, which would be required as a result of a reputation crisis.

DOI: 10.1057/9781137547378.0007

17   Weeks 2015. Any organization needs to assess whether the profile of the
      issue is high or low in the media; it subsequently needs to analyze the ratio
      of positive versus detracting messages that were negative for VW during
      the 2012–2013 period. Next the firm needs to understand the context in
      which messages are framed (personal safety in case of VW 2013; the poor
      engagement with the public did not help it either). Finally, it then assesses
      the emotional representation of the issue (the powerful fear/anxiety in the
      case of VW 2013) that may have a significant impact on the firm's financial
      performance.

18   Gardner 2015: 80–81. Some easy heuristic rules to establish worthy
      partnership across borders need to be followed: (1) do not squeeze your tem
      members; (2) deliver what you committed to on time, without reminders;
      and (3) communicate openly.

19   The eBay website states:

      > eBay is a community that encourages open and honest communication among all
      > its members. Our community is guided by five fundamental values: (1) We believe
      > people are basically good; (2) we believe everyone has something to contribute; (3)
      > we believe that an honest, open environment can bring out the best in people; (4)
      > we recognize and respect everyone as a unique individual; (5) we encourage you to
      > treat others the way you want to be treated. eBay is firmly committed to these prin-
      > ciples. And we believe that community members should also honor them – whether
      > buying, selling, or chatting with eBay friends.

20   Reichheld 2006b.

21   According to Wikipedia, the *Net Promoter* or *Net Promoter Score (NPS)* is a
      management tool that can be used to gauge the loyalty of a firm's customer
      relationships. It serves as an alternative to traditional customer satisfaction
      research and claims to be correlated with revenue growth. "Net Promoter
      Score" is a customer loyalty metric developed by (and a registered trademark
      of) Fred Reichheld, Bain & Company and Satmetrix. It was introduced
      by professor Reichheld in his 2006 *Harvard Business Review* article "One
      Number You Need to Grow." NPS can be as low as −100 (everybody is a
      detractor) or as high as +100 (everybody is a promoter). An NPS that is
      positive (i.e., higher than zero) is felt to be good, and an NPS of +50 is
      excellent. Net Promoter Score (NPS) measures the loyalty that exists between
      a provider and a consumer. The provider can be a company, employer or
      any other entity. The provider is the entity that is asking the questions on the
      NPS survey. The consumer is the customer, employee or respondent to an
      NPS survey.

22   Reichheld 2006b: 17–20. The NPS is based on the fundamental perspective that
      every company's customers can be divided into three categories. Promoters
      are loyal enthusiasts who keep buying from a company and urge their friends
      to do the same. Passives are satisfied but unenthusiastic customers who can
      be easily wooed by the competition. And detractors are unhappy customers

trapped in a bad relationship. Customers can be categorized according to their answer to the (ultimate) question. Those who answer nine or ten on a zero-to-ten scale, for instance, are promoters, and so on.

23   Reichheld 2006b: 20.

24   Reichheld 2006a. The aim of NPS is to unravel the mystery of loyal versus angry customers. The following characteristics need to be analyzed: (1) the retention rate indicating how long a customer stays with the company; (2) margins: promoters are usually less price-sensitive because they believe in the good value from the company; (3) annual spend: promoters' interest in new product offerings and brand extensions far exceeds that of detractors or passives; (4) cost efficiencies: detractors complain more frequently, thereby consuming customer-services resources. Some companies also find that credit losses are higher for detractors; (5) word of mouth: promoters account for 80–90 percent of positive referrals (i.e., reputation), and most of the lifetime value of these new customers should be allocated to promoters.

25   Reichheld 2006a, 2006b.

26   Kim & Mauborgne 2014.

27   Kim & Mauborgne 2014; Verhezen 2015. When employees value leadership practices, they in effect buy into this leadership. They are likely inspired to excel and act with commitment. However, when employees do not buy the existing leadership, they disengage, becoming noncustomers of the current leadership style. Thinking about leadership in this way allows to see that the concepts and frameworks of Blue Ocean to create new demand by converting noncustomers into customers could be adapted to help leaders convert disengaged employees into engaged ones.

28   Kim & Mauborgne 2014 provide evidence of their framework with the example of an English retailer who applied blue ocean leadership to redefine what effectiveness meant for frontline, midlevel, and senior leaders. The impact was significant. On the frontline, for example, employee turnover dropped from about 40 percent to 11 percent in the first year, reducing recruitment and training costs by 50 percent. Factoring in reduced absenteeism, the group saved more than $50 million in the first year, while customer satisfaction scores climbed by over 30 percent.

29   Charan 2015: 117–126.

30   See http://www.umicore.com/en/

31   Bazerman 2014. There are a number of factors that contribute to be too relax on certain behavior that seems to be justifiable despite the slippery slope.

32   Bazerman & Tenbrunsel 2011.

33   Mackey & Sisodia 2013.

34   This notion of blended value that combines business and social objectives in a blended manner has been quipped by Emerson in a 2003 paper.

35   Waddock 2008

DOI: 10.1057/9781137547378.0007

36 Kim 2014.
37 Eccles & Serafeim 2013.
38 Henderson 2015.
39 Visit their website: http://methodhome.com/about-us/our-story/
40 Radjou & Prahbu 2015: 80–82.
41 Radjou & Prahbu 2015.
42 Radjou & Prahbu 2015.
43 Phillips, Freeman & Wicks 2003; Phillips 2003; Freeman 1984. A firm's
    legitimate or normative stakeholders are those groups to whom the firm
    owes an obligation because these stakeholders are willing to cooperate
    with the firm to address their concerns. We have labeled those legitimate
    or *engaged* stakeholders. In other words, proponents of the Stakeholder
    Theory such as Ed Freeman will argue that there is no contradiction between
    shareholders and stakeholders. In fact, it sounds quite like Porter's notion of
    Corporate Shared Value where business interests are completely aligned with
    societal objectives.

DOI: 10.1057/9781137547378.0007

4
Boards Acting Wisely: Be Different, Beyond Compliance

Abstract: *Governance is more than compliance; it reflects a culture or attitude that embraces consistency, responsibility, accountability, fairness, transparency and respect for shareholders' rights and stakeholders' concerns. Governance and reputation management are correlated. The more a board is able to fulfill its fiduciary duties of loyalties and care, the less reputational risk and possibly the higher the reputation of the organization. Good governance provides the check and balances to control risks and to prepare organizations to embrace opportunities. A board promotes and communicates the central idea of why the company exists and how the company will collaborate and compete ethically and win. Boards have evolved from rubber-stamping to monitoring and control, though some excellent boards are now taking a more active leading and coaching role.*

Verhezen, Peter. *The Vulnerability of Corporate Reputation: Leadership for Sustainable Long-Term Value.* Basingstoke: Palgrave Macmillan, 2015. DOI: 10.1057/9781137547378.0008.

When it comes to running a business that achieves optimal returns for investors, governing boards, employees and customers, bottom-line-driven leaders rarely deliver the goods. After all the debacles and crises, people seem to be hungry for some meaningful shift toward responsibility and accountability in leadership. Leadership that has the **character** to take wise decisions will make that difference. The character[1] of those enlightened leaders is revealed all the time through observable behavior, by internalizing the moral principles of a society and achieving a mature level of autonomous self-awareness and self-esteem. Moreover, one cannot legislate *character,* nor its attributes *integrity*, *courage*, *resilience* and *compassion*. It must come from inside the corporation; it requires a leadership with the highest ethical standards. Boards act with integrity when their communication and actions are consistent with their intentions. A lack of integrity is at best hypocrisy and at worst lying, not exactly trustworthy behavior. Building trust requires nothing more than telling the truth. Spinning the truth attempts to give the appearance of concern for these key stakeholders when the leadership were actually acting out of self-concern, not exactly showing great character.

4.1   Having a meaningful purpose in business

Being a corporate leader or CEO is mostly about making decisions that will benefit the organization. The strength of a leader's *character* seems to be an important driver for business success. Making wise decisions is an innate ability for leadership to draw on available knowledge to discern a situation or relationships and develop qualities to act in a meaningful manner that contributes to value creation for the organization.[2] Such virtuous leaders communicate ***what*** the organization is doing and ***why*** it is doing it.

Organizations do not change themselves. Leaders change organizations. And wise leaders who have the character to translate a compelling vision into a workable and focused strategy may change an organization in a positive manner. In such a case, leadership almost always creates a culture of accountability and responsibility. "You can easily judge the character of a man by how he treats those who can do nothing for him," Goethe, the great 19th-century German thinker, poet and scientist, eloquently expressed it. In other words, character describes the values incorporated in the behavior of individuals. If character describes how a leader thinks

DOI: 10.1057/9781137547378.0008

and acts, then the culture in an organization reflects the character of a group of employees and how they as a collective thank and act.[3]

The subsequent question then is *to whom* and *for what* leaders are accountable. Obviously, corporate leaders are accountable to their board, who look after the interest of the organization. Leaders and top executives have a *fiduciary duty* and ethical responsibility to those whose capital has been trusted to their care, and such a fiduciary duty expresses a legal relationship of trust between a principal or beneficiary and a fiduciary or trustee. Fulfilling the fiduciary duty may not have a dramatic effect on the corporate reputation; excelling the expectations does. As argued, the shareholder may be the main principal to whom boards and leadership are ultimately accountable, but customers' and employees' rights and community's concerns should be taken into account as well. And what about investors who own shares for a few seconds when trading stock? The investor psychology changes dramatically, turning prudent owners into rent-seeking trendy consumers of stock.[4] Short-term owners do not necessarily act like owners but rather like renters maximizing short-term profitability irrespective of whether that benefits the organization or not.

Wise decision making implies that leaders have developed not only character but also the ability to reason in paradoxes, transcending the simple *either-or* with a more complex *both-and* thinking. Empirical data seem to suggest that high-character leaders at the end of the top of the curve created a return on assets nearly five times greater than did the self-focused CEOs at the bottom of the curve.[5] And that higher return on assets translated into a reputation of trustworthy leaders who have shown good ethical behavior while performing superbly.

The "oracle of Omaha," Warren Buffet, is such a man who has gained that status of a "wise," fair and extremely effective investor. A good practitioner is usually motivated to aim at a meaningful purpose of his practice. Therefore, acting wisely demands that leaders are guided by goals that feel meaningful. That is why working for monetary incentives is not the same as working to achieve a meaningful *purpose* of an activity.

Famous business leaders such as Herb Keller of Southwest Airlines (1) employed positive abundance thinking that gives people a dream to believe in and to materialize, instead of being limited to think in terms of pure scarcity; (2) used confidence, honesty and reasonableness in their decision making; (3) maintained a philosophy of inclusiveness instead of exclusiveness; and (4) made "risky" choices to overcome high barriers

DOI: 10.1057/9781137547378.0008

to enter the airline business.[6] Analyzing any successful business leader will reveal some characteristics of being competent, having the resilience and integrity to resist temptation and being courageous to make difficult choices. That makes a leader being trusted by shareholders and stakeholders alike.

Relying on formalistic corporate governance rules and pecuniary corporate incentives only may *crowd out* wise decision making and its commitment to embrace a higher "common" purpose. Research reveals that it is often better to minimize the number of rules, give up trying to cover every particular circumstance and instead do more training to encourage skills at practical reasoning and intuition.[7] Practical wisdom[8] combines *will* with *skill*. However, skill without will – without the desire to achieve a meaningful activity – can lead to manipulation of others. Reliance on pecuniary incentives often undermines moral *will*. Moreover, rigid and detailed rules can undermine the development and deployment of moral *skill* – the other crucial component of practical wisdom. It means that the traditional "motivators" of rules and incentives demoralize both the practices that rely on them and the practitioners engaged in those practices.[9] Effective leadership understands how to make choices that are consistent with the evolving goals and objectives of the firm. Indeed, practical wisdom remains an ongoing, finite and fallible process, reaching out to what can be aspired to.

In promoting collaboration, wise decision makers and mentors should focus on *motivation* rather than mere *talent*. Motivation[10] or will is much more difficult to teach. Some people call it "grit," "resilience" or "persistence," which are the passion and perseverance toward long-term goals to undertake all endeavors to achieve that goal. Gritty people – above and beyond intelligence and aptitude – often achieve higher performance by virtue of their interest, focus and drive. Of course, natural talent matters, but persistence is a major factor that predicts how close someone can materialize their full potential. And there seems to be a close connection between *grit* and *giving*. Resilient leaders who understand the importance of meaningful giving are usually well aware that such "giving" can energize rather than exhaust. Such conditional giving also signals to others that one is "good" and trustworthy, providing reputational benefits. Consequently, such (conditional) generous leaders are more likely to move to the top in making sustainable contributions to the group or the organization. As Simon Sinek writes, "Givers advance the world. Takers advance themselves and hold the world back."[11]

DOI: 10.1057/9781137547378.0008

Professor Adam Grant found in his research that givers are willing to work harder and longer than takers and matchers because of their dedication to others. Often they do so out of a sense of responsibility to their team.[12] In selecting and promoting motivated talent, one of the prevailing qualities leaders would look for would be the ability and the possible commitment to be able to give. For one simple reason: those givers will enable teams to collaborate and to fulfill their potential, and hence can significantly improve the chances of success in groups and organizations.

The idea that the only responsibility of a board and its executive leadership is to maximize profits for its investors and capital providers has been labeled the *Agency Theory*.[13] However, companies are not necessarily the "vassals" of their shareholders, as this prevailing Agency Theory assumes. And these shareholders do not own the business, just the shares of the business. The formal residual rights of those shareholders extend only to the appointment of board members, and in case of bankruptcy or liquidation access to the assets of the business after all other claimants have been paid. Moreover, the responsibilities of the directors are to the organization as a whole, not to the shareholders alone as is sometimes wrongly assumed. "It was a widespread misinterpretation of company law that gave rise to the elevation of shareholder value as the prime [and almost sole] purpose of the company, to short thinking and the splurge of business tied to share performance [only]."[14] Moreover, it is not scientifically proven over a longer period that adhering to the Shareholder or Agency Theory has provided superior financial results. Rothmans Business School professor Roger Martin has calculated that, overall, company profits were lower in the 40 years after 1970 (adhering to the Agency Theory) than they were in the 40 years before, when managers were paid normal salaries to do their job.[15] We may even argue that in some instances over that longer period we have moved from value creation to value extraction by the top management.

The assumptions of the underlying self(ish) interest in this neoclassical economic framework of the *Homo Oeconomicus* that underwrites the Agency Model seem to be quite detached from reality.[16] Justifying an unregulated pursuit of mere self-interest as enlightened social policy or organizational optimization policy may be far-fetched and does not even describe economic reality. In other words, the assumption that an economy is driven purely by selfish rational agents, guided by an "invisible hand" that benefits the common good, may be quite a powerful

DOI: 10.1057/9781137547378.0008

metaphor, but it does not correspond to reality. Unrestrained self-interest is self-destructive and unsustainable over a longer period, and is likely to undermine the common good, by profiting some members of the society at the expense of others. Ultimately, such "selfish" behavior negatively affects corporate reputation. Business is part of a community. Community members belong to such a community but do now possess or own the community. As the word "company" suggests, they are "companions" and are more properly regarded as citizens with responsibilities as well as rights, rather than as paid employees or "human resources" that can be used and dismissed at any time.

Governance is more than compliance. Good corporate governance is a **culture** of consistency, responsibility, accountability, fairness, transparency, deference to (shareholders' and stakeholders') rights and effectiveness that is deployed throughout the organization. That implies that governance must be "managed" as a cultural phenomenon.[17] And when corporate culture helps and does not hinder the firm to achieve its strategy and its business objectives, *reputation and governance are positively correlated*.

When corporate governance has been reduced to the minimum bureaucracy required to comply and to 'tick all the boxes', rather than 'how we do things around here', risks of reputation inevitably increase. In a healthy governance ecosystem, there is an integrated balance between the board, shareholders, management and the other important stakeholders who can affect the value of the organization. An imbalance can undermine the integrative health and vibrancy and direction of the entire organization. Governance is more than a bureaucratic box-ticking exercise.

Reputation risk and good corporate governance are inversely correlated. The more a board is able to fulfill its fiduciary duties, the higher the reputation of the organization. When corporate culture and strategy are aligned through appropriate governance structures and mechanisms, the potential risk of reputational disasters is greatly diminished. The role of governance here aims to produce and enforce rules, structures and processes that align a firm's operating procedures and strategy to improve performance. Therefore, good governance principles of transparency, fairness, equal shareholders' rights, accountability and responsibility provide the check and balances to control risks (on the downside) and to prepare organizations to embrace opportunities (on the upside) in a reasonable manner as visualized in Figure 4.1.

Building and preserving trust is necessary to create or enhance reputation. And to keep this kind of trust, what matters most are what the philosopher David Hume has labeled "correct sentiments, imagination, and cooperative genius." In other words, virtuous leadership could enable employees to materialize their full potential of productivity and to provide real solutions and worthy experiences to customers and the community at large. But then again, corporate governance can be interpreted as an exercise in minimally complying to the legal rules and regulations, or can be defined as "doing the right thing, always," embracing the fiduciary accountability to its capital providers and the ethical and ecological responsibility to its concerned and dedicated stakeholders, including the community in which the organization physically operates or affects. In other words, "best" corporate governance practices and standards embrace more holistic organizational objectives, whereas a more narrow legal interpretation of the fiduciary duties is accounted for only to its shareholders, as made visual in Figure 4.1. And because values, norms and regulations continuously shift to higher standards, the "letter of the law" and the "spirit of the law" will likely push up the expectations imposed on the organization. What was "acceptable" yesterday may not

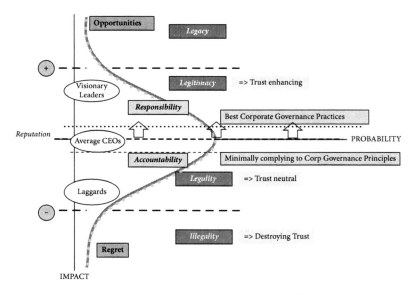

FIGURE 4.1   *Fiduciary accountability and ethical responsibility*
Source: Design by Verhezen 2015.

DOI: 10.1057/9781137547378.0008

be anymore tomorrow; leaders have no choice but to adopt to this pressing and often ambiguous reality.

Merely complying with the minimal rules and regulations keeps the organization's legal liability to a minimum. But corporate governance practices refer to the system of check and balances instituted by the board of directors to ensure that an organization is equipped to meet its overall business objectives, aligned with broader societal objectives. Good corporate governance does not just maximize the interests of insiders. Since **corporate reputation is the perception of the firm by a variety of stakeholders**, board members should consider having an organizational oversight program in place to ensure that corporate behavior does not compromise the company's ability to achieve its long-term goals.

4.2 Transparency beyond compliance; motivating beyond pecuniary rewards

Boards appreciate the importance of enterprise risk management (ERM) as a reputation risk management tool. Directors should embed reputation risk into an enterprise risk management system, fostering a cohesive culture of risk awareness. It is common sense to prioritize stakeholder relations. In addition, boards oversee the process adopted by senior executives to identify, categorize and prioritize business uncertainties with respect to their reputation effects. And overseeing the determination of a proper response strategy to each risk category affecting corporate reputation is a must to govern such risks.

Assessing the gaps and vulnerability in the existing reputation risk management solutions should not be overlooked. Most likely, it also means that the board needs to reemphasize the underlying mission and discuss reputation enhancement as a program objective. A governance framework determines the response strategies to risk events and reputation effects and selects assessment techniques and defines risk appetite and tolerance. Wisely choosing compensation policies and performance metrics to promote and track the pursuit of long-term reputation capital is not to be overlooked.

Besides the almost exclusive focus on risk avoidance, boards often take an inside-out perspective on threats, instead of being open to outside-in approaches. Moreover, searching for what is "new" out there and reflecting on what it could mean to the organization will help to view the

DOI: 10.1057/9781137547378.0008

business in a different light and potentially spark innovative ideas for new growth trajectories. Such outside-in perspective will require organizations to expand their networks, relationships and sources of information far beyond the company's core competencies and the understanding of the industry.

The board should, indeed, be aware of the negative risks and potential liabilities in using social media, but it should also see the potential opportunities and advantages.[18] *It is the board's responsibility to ensure that the firm has a comprehensive social media strategy and policies.* When are social media practices beneficial for the company's information transparency and disclosure policies? When could those damage the firm's image or even raise some legal risk by disclosing unnecessary information?[19] Having a proper crisis management and crisis procedures in place helps boards and executive management to mitigate some of those risks. Stakeholders are asking more and more responsible behavior from organizations: ethics and working conditions as well as the organizational culture take on a new importance since employees have become *de facto* examiners of the company, potentially putting it in the public spotlight.

Boards are well aware about the importance of good corporate governance when dealing with reputation in connection with the emergence of social media. Indeed, a *new level of transparency* will make organizations more accountable in the eyes of the public. Boards should assess how the organization's vision, actions and values are being perceived by the public and decide whether corrective actions need to be taken. Second, *empowered stakeholders* have reduced the disparity of power that companies wield through traditional media. Smart companies and their boards use the symbiotic relationship between social and "old" media by creating inexpensive social media marketing campaigns. Third, the *rise of e-lobbying and e-advocacy* by NGOs or activist shareholders, for instance, to influence corporations demonstrate the wide power of those critical criticizing groups. Unhappy critical stakeholders can organize strikes or product boycotts. Moreover, social media can create a domino effect as long as an "accepted truth" is endorsed and acted upon by the public. Fourth, the *immediacy of social media* can give as much exposure to lies as to truths. Any opinion or information (true or false) can go viral in a matter of hours. If wisely used, social media users could become allies in defending the company's product or image. Finally, the availability of social media gives smaller and medium-sized companies too the opportunity to potentially reach a clientele or interest group that would otherwise have been very expensive. In other words, social media gives a *level-playing field* for all business firms, potentially increasing the competition as well as collaboration between organizations.

Just relying on monetary incentives, however, may not optimize the potential of the human capabilities in the organization. Short-term thinking and at the same time performance distortion were encouraged by "corporate governance" systems in the United States and other Western capital markets. Perceived self-determination and self-esteem suffer from external interventions in the form of external monetary incentives. As a result, individuals may shift their intrinsic motivation drivers to outside pecuniary rewards. Their attention shifts from the activity itself to the monetary reward. Therefore, intrinsically motivated integrity or honesty can be undermined by the presumption that agent managers act solely in the interests of the shareholders if they are paid enough to do so. The unfortunate effect is that a *monetary compensation may reduce the voluntary commitment* to the firm and even its shareholders. This monetary and even symbolic compensation can easily *crowd out* civic virtue or other intrinsic motivators.[20]

Extrinsic motivation refers to doing something because it leads to a separable outcome; employees are motivated because of an instrumental monetized value. Many executives and entrepreneurs are not necessarily motivated by just money but rather by pursuing an *inspiring purpose* and by giving *meaning* to their business. It is hard to overestimate the power of *intrinsic motivators,*[21] which provides a feeling of accomplishment and of learning, of being a key player on a team that is achieving something meaningful. Intrinsic motivation refers to doing something as in a free choice because it is inherently interesting or enjoyable. The system – especially investors' analysts who work on behalf of institutional investors – often seems to reward senior executives for being decidedly focused on the short term,[22] inadvertently undermining the company's purpose, long-term goals and objectives. This *short-termism* is especially true for low-growth sectors such as insurance, retail, pharmaceutical, telecom and financial trading where growth has been marginal. Once leadership has formulated a viable strategy, investors "should be impatient for growth and patient for profit."[23] Unfortunately, almost half of the CEOs of Fortune 500 companies claim that their boards and institutional investors put pressure to deliver strong short-term financial performance.[24] Too many of those players are not really acting like owners who

DOI: 10.1057/9781137547378.0008

have the foresight to prepare for long-term value. Institutional investors and boards that focus on short-term are failing to engage with their corporate leaders to shape the organization's long-term course. This trend among institutional investors who press boards and their corporate leaders can be reversed only by (1) redefining the organization's risk appetite and long-term objectives aligned to its purpose; (2) engaging in long-term relationship building with the board and corporate leadership to cooperate with industry coalitions that seek to foster wise investment that embraces ESG issues; and (3) having the proper institutionalized governance structures and mechanisms in place that support a long-term approach.[25] A longer-term approach is often correlated to the ultimate purpose or the intrinsic motivator of an organization answering the compelling question of *why they are doing what they do*.

When managers and employees identify organizational values, through integration and alignment of corporate and individual values, or even through external governance regulation,[26] the monetary extrinsic motivators do not necessarily fully crowd out the intrinsic motivators.[27] Technically speaking, professor Benabou and Nobel Prize winner professor Tirole argue that as long as the *trust effect* outweighs the profitability effect, there does not need to occur such a crowding out effect.[28] A specific meaningful organizational context – reflected by its corporate reputation and trust – could support intrinsic motivation, but can also be facilitated by internationalization and integration of extrinsic motivated tasks. In other words, meaning and monetary incentive systems can reinforce each other under the right circumstances in which rewards and punishments are meticulously and fairly "aligned." A board taking wise decisions also promotes and communicates the central idea of *why* the company exists and *how* the company will compete ethically and win. Boards have evolved from rubber-stamping to monitoring and control, while some excellent boards are now taking leading role, which means that the boundaries between directing and managing are shifting too.[29] Boards define the dividing lines between a shared reality, mutual respect, performance and the alignment of all the values and goals.

Maybe some "crowding in" of intrinsic motivation can be boosted by perceived autonomy, perceived competence and social relatedness. It is therefore strongly suggested that the decision-making process of an organization strengthens *participation and self-governance*. Organizations with a clear distinctive purpose can inspire their employees and excite customers. Succinctly communicating a unique and distinctive value

DOI: 10.1057/9781137547378.0008

proposition to its potential customers, supported by tailored value chain activities and founded by governance mechanisms that express the organizational purpose, are the necessary ingredients for a viable strategy.

Stricter control and the threat of negative sanctions tend to decrease loyalty to the firm. Intrinsic motivation to behave honestly tends to be crowded out all the more if a large number of the members of the organization are acting dishonestly. This is the unfortunate fate of some public officials with high integrity in corrupt organizations in countries with weak institutions; ironically, they are often ostracized within their own institution. Hence it is often argued that managers must be paid a "fair" market wage in exchange for their overall performance, reducing the temptations to consciously or unconsciously cheat the firm.[30]

In the light of what we have discussed so far, it might be wiser to aim to grow better without necessary bigger.[31] Giving any reasonable forecast of future eco-efficiency gain, GDP growth will have to be modified, if we are to avoid the depletion of all ecosystems on this planet. Currently, economic growth measures are measures of quantity instead of suggested measures of quality. The role of business is not just to enrich the capital providers, but to help employees, customers and the community in which it operates to flourish. Economic growth then could be a means to a greater purpose rather than an end in itself. There is always a bigger picture.

Notes

1   Kiel 2015: 17. Character is defined as "an individual's unique combination of internalized beliefs and moral habits that motivate and shape how that individual relates to others."

2   Sternberg 2003; Jones 2005. Knowing one's self is the *conditio sine qua non* to reach some level of wisdom. The components of wisdom are described as: (1) A high level of consciousness. Becoming aware of their own qualities and relationships of all life forms; (2) Power of choice. Wise people recognize through introspection that they, and by logical extension all humans, have been endowed with an inner quality that can be referred to as the power of choice, (3) Internal locus of control. A wise person will choose his response to external events that may be beyond his control, rather than allow external events to direct his life; (4) Awareness of self-fulfilling prophecy. To avoid having no control over fate, a person must become aware that operating

DOI: 10.1057/9781137547378.0008

in high consciousness is a choice that can be made by each individual; (5) Inclusiveness. Inclusive people are aware that all of Life is interconnected; they include all of Life in their thoughts and consider all of Life when making choices; (6) Abundance. A wise person in high consciousness will choose to operate from the perspective of abundance and believe that all problems can be worked out. Taking the perspective of inclusiveness and abundance is congruent with further choices to be honest, logical and reasonable and this allows wise people to live in *harmony* with all Life; and (7) A decision process that is guided by honesty, logic and reasonableness.

3   Sinek 2009 & 2013.

4   Young 2015.

5   Kiel 2015.

6   Jones 2005.

7   Weick's research on firefighters and the destructive effects of rules and incentives to make "wise" decisions that save the life of people, quoted in Schwartz 2011.

8   Verhezen 2013. Tentatively, we here define *managerial wisdom* as an ability that enables leaders and executives to minimize the cognitive limitations of bounded rational capabilities by relying on (1) (cognitive and affective) knowledge or skills; (2) long individual or organizational experience that functions as a tradition; (3) intellectual and moral virtues that constitute the will of a person, which underpins managerial decisions; and finally (4) an openness to continuously learn to improve, resulting in heuristically fallible best decisions or actions.

9   Schwartz 2011, 17.

10   Pink 2009.

11   Sinek 2013.

12   Grant 2013: 119.

13   Jensen & Meckling 1976; Jensen 1986, 2002.

14   Handy 2015: 100.

15   Quoted in Handy 2015: 100–101.

16   Wilson 2015.

17   Tucker 2011: 17. To establish a correlation between reputation risk and good governance, one must interpret governance as "organizational culture." Culture, as Edgar Schein defines it, is "a pattern of shared tacit assumptions that was learned by a group as it solved its problems of external adaptation and internal integration, that has worked well enough to be considered valid, and, therefore, to be taught to new members as the correct way to perceive, think, and feel in relation to these problems."

18   We use the excellent paper by Chaher and Spellman 2011 to summarize the crucial points that boards should focus on in "steering" their organizations to deal with social media.

DOI: 10.1057/9781137547378.0008

19 Verhezen 2015, Silver 2012. In the *Signal and the Noise*, Nate Silver examines the world of prediction, investigating how we can distinguish a true signal (such as indications of corporate success) from a universe of noisy, ever-increasing data and irrelevant gossip. Increased scrutiny by the social media has pushed boards to study and to understand how the company is perceived in the social media, while at the same time being aware that there is much "noise" generated by multiple channels and sources.

20 Osterloh & Frey 2004.

21 Christensen, Allworth & Dillon 2012. The authors argue that any strategy – either for individuals or for a corporation – will need to focus on maximizing the intrinsic motivators which give purpose and meaning to the job, while satisfying the hygiene factors or extrinsic motivators (such as status, compensation, job security, work conditions, company policies and supervisory practices). On the basis of these intrinsic and extrinsic motivators, a strategy will likely emerge from a combination of deliberate and unanticipated opportunities.

22 Lev 2012. Clearly, there are short-term-oriented investors. However, the assertion that those short-termers would dominate capital markets to the extent that managers have to shape corporate strategies and decisions that sacrifice future value to accommodate them is overrated. It is true in capital markets that long term is a succession of short terms in that good management caters simultaneously to the short and long term.

23 Christensen, Allworth & Dillon 2012: 88.

24 Barton & Wiseman 2015.

25 Barton & Wiseman 2015: 224. The authors conclude that
today a strong desire exists in many business circles to move beyond quarterly capitalism. But short-term mind-sets still prevail throughout the investment value chain and dominate decisions in boardrooms. [...] moving this debate from ideas to action is with the people who provide the essential fuel for capitalism – the world's major asset owners. [...] large asset owners can be a powerful force for instituting the kind of balanced, long-term capitalism that ultimately benefits everyone.

26 Ryan & Deci 2000.

27 Frey 1997.

28 Benabou & Tirole 2003: 503–504. "Rewards can impact intrinsic motivation. Whereas under symmetric information the intrinsic and extrinsic motivations can be clearly separated, under asymmetric information they cannot. When the agent is unsure about his ability, the intrinsic motivation decreases with the level of the bonus. Similarly, when he does not know how costly or exciting the task is, his perception of it is affected by the level of the wage or reward." However, a reward can be a positive reinforcer in the short term, but almost always decreases future motivation. This confirms the "crowding out" effect over a longer period, whereby workers' behavior that is controlled via incentives as "alienating" and "dehumanizing" over a longer

DOI: 10.1057/9781137547378.0008

period. And focusing on rewards change the "focus of causality from internal to external, making employees bored, alienated and reactive rather than proactive."

29   Charan, Carey & Useem 2014; Verhezen 2013.

30   Osterloh & Frey 2004.

31   Handy 2015. Maybe economies of scale could be achieved by noncompetitive alliances, by working together without necessarily controlling.

DOI: 10.1057/9781137547378.0008

Concluding Remarks: The Vulnerability of Corporate Reputation

Abstract: *Reputation is one of the most undervalued but nonetheless crucial organizational assets. A good corporate reputation can lead to numerous benefits such as lower costs, competitive barriers that enable firms to charge a premium price, to obtain improved credit rating, to attract better employees and to retain more loyal customers, all translating into improved performance and increased profitability. Reputation also provides clear signals to others about intentions or activities. The notion of reputation can be a touchstone that enables leadership to change strategic direction according to sound norms and structures of governance.*

Four generic recommendations aim to create, enhance or preserve corporate reputation: (1) communicating a corporate narrative based on a meaningful purpose versus short-termism; (2) collaborative innovation versus self-focused competitive advantage at all costs; (3) caring for "people, planet and profit" versus shareholder value maximization; and (4) governing responsibly beyond compliance versus minimally interpreted fiduciary accountability.

Wise and resilient leadership built on appropriate foundations of good corporate governance usually performs better over a longer period. Despite the importance of corporate reputation, it remains vulnerable and dependent on outside perspectives.

Verhezen, Peter. *The Vulnerability of Corporate Reputation: Leadership for Sustainable Long-Term Value.* Basingstoke: Palgrave Macmillan, 2015. DOI: 10.1057/9781137547378.0009.

Refocusing on reputation is potentially a very practical way for business leaders to strike a better and more sustainable compromise between the narrow expectations of financial markets and the broader expectations of the world at large. This approach would refine the nature, values and profile of organizations by explicitly relating the internal structure, strategies and culture to the external environment and a wide range of stakeholders.

Reputation is arguably one of the most undervalued but nonetheless crucial organizational assets. Reputation is an intangible asset that helps the firm to exploit opportunities and to defend itself against threats. Being intangible, rare and difficult to imitate, reputation can also be a source of competitive advantage and enhanced profitability.[1] A good corporate reputation can lead to numerous benefits such as lower costs, competitive barriers that enable firms to charge a premium price, to obtain improved credit rating, to attract better employees and to retain more loyal customers, all translating into improved performance and increased profitability. Reputation also provides clear *signals* to others about intentions or activities.[2] The notion of reputation can be a touchstone that enables leadership to change strategic direction according to the sound norms and structures of governance.

C.1   Ways to create, enhance or preserve corporate reputation

This book so far has attempted to clarify the nature of corporate reputation and explain *why* it is becoming more important to successful business. Constructively engaging in an open dialogue with investors and key stakeholders may allow leadership and boards to better realize strategies that enhance sustainable long-term value.

This concluding chapter considers *how* business leaders can transcend the constraints of short-termism, misaligned incentives and unsubstantiated market fetishism and relax the market-driven tyranny of distorted accounting and its obsession with the pseudo-clarity of accounting numbers. Wise choices build reputation and minimize reputational risks. These four generic recommendations, derived from the preceding chapters, summarize the governance imperative in relation to good corporate reputation.

DOI: 10.1057/9781137547378.0009

C.1.1   A corporate narrative of a meaningful purpose versus overregulation and short-termism

Long-term sustainability requires alignment of a company's values with its evolving social context. Most organizations today are over-managed and under-led. Truly great companies like Unilever and Nestle[3] are more than mere money machines; they combine financial and social logic to build enduring success. These great organizations invest in the future while being aware of the needs of critical key stakeholders and society at large. One predominant characteristic of endearing organizations is their engrained meaningful purpose aligned with long-term vision of what is a sustainable organization. That vision and purpose then is translated into daily activities of the organization. PepsiCo's aspiring "Performance with Purpose," for instance – making nutrition and environmental responsibility a core value – provides strategic direction and motivation for their activities. It guides PepsiCo to reduce or eliminate sugar and sodium in food and beverages. And it provides an identity for the people who work at PepsiCo.

Purpose-driven leaders do not just manage, they persuade. They do not execute initiatives; they lead fans.[4] A truly *purpose-driven* company that is customer-centric and engages with employees lives up to the Golden Rule. Indeed, employees treat customers the way they would want to be treated. Experience shows that "profitable" customers who are loyal are "happy" customers who promote the cause of the organization. Ask any Harley Davidson or Apple fan. Nothing bonds a team more than a shared purpose, a common cause. The more the key stakeholders – be it employees, customers, investors or suppliers – share this meaningful purpose or cause, the more satisfying the engagement will be.

However, the very presence of short-term financial goals may lead top management and employees to focus efficiently but myopically on short-term gains and to lose sight of the potential devastating long-term effects on the organization. The global financial crisis in 2008–2009 made that very clear. What seems to be "irrational exuberance" is ultimately nothing but a bad case of distorted incentive systems base on myopic short-term profitability. Indeed, short-termism undermines the ability to invest in exploring new business opportunities that take time to translate in commercially viable projects. Those missed investments, in turn, have far-reaching consequences for our economy, be it slower GDP growth, higher employment and lower return on investment. Companies

DOI: 10.1057/9781137547378.0009

like Unilever have decided to forego quarterly expectation reports and have made it clear that they cater for long-term investors who believe in their Sustainable Plan. Other companies such as IKEA have declined the tempting opportunity to list their company and decided to remain privately held, enabling them to ignore short-termism and focus on the sustainability of providing "affordable design furniture to everyone." Doing something that matters, doing it well and doing it in the service of a cause, larger than the individual, is usually very meaningful and makes perfect business sense. Communicating the reasons *why* provides stakeholders the context in which the organization wishes to operate.

The corporate's aim is not to choose profits while trying to stay ethical and law-abiding. But the goal is to pursue a meaningful purpose and use profit as a catalyst rather than an objective. When leaders resist the pressure by short-term investors and focus on the sensible reasons *why* they are doing *what* they do so well, it could institutionalize a more balanced form of decision making that ultimately benefits everyone. There is no stronger message to investors and other dedicated stakeholders than transparently communicating a genuine narrative that is credible as in pursuing the "right" goals of a meaningful purpose, while avoiding any form of greenwashing. Understanding the true purpose of an organization – the why – is crucial to be successful and sustainable. Good leaders truly care about those entrusted to their (fiduciary) care. Only then a leader will be able to inspire others to do more and become more.

Achieving a more sustainable organization that transcends short-termism implies that its leaders identify and incorporate (reputational) risks from "stranded" assets that may lose significant value well ahead of their anticipated useful life span as a result of changes in regulations, legislation, market forces, disruptive innovation, societal norms, values shifts, or environmental shocks.[5] Boards and its leadership may also opt to internally mandate integrated reporting that addresses a more comprehensive insight into companies, aligning financial and ESG performance into one report.

Another obstacle to achieve corporate (reputational) excellence is the excessive financial rewards to top executives. *Some of those outsized remuneration packages are exaggerated as if one person or a small team is solely responsible for the overall performance of the organization and its reputation.* Obviously, wise leadership can make a difference and should be remunerated accordingly. But driving a hierarchical remuneration wig between the top and its subordinates may not be the wisest decision.

DOI: 10.1057/9781137547378.0009

Too big inequality within a cohesive group has never proven to excel, especially over a longer period. Moreover, one could also encourage to align compensation structures with long-term sustainable performance, employing rolling multiyear milestones for performance evaluation. And taking a stance against mere algorithmic and very short-term trading by a communication strategy focused on highlighting long-term value creation and potentially using financial instruments rewarding "patient" capital may be worth considering. Leading companies are using sustainability to create operations' and strategic advantages, to boost their corporate reputation.

C.1.2 Collaborative innovation versus self-focused competitive advantage at all costs

People and institutions that have developed well-regarded reputations can more easily cooperate or benefit from the characteristic of being more credible than others, either as a possible deterrence to follow up on a threat or to improve the chances that same-liked people or organizations get involved in reciprocal relationships. In other words, *reputation can enhance cooperation by giving people incentives to demonstrate their willingness to cooperate or intolerance for free-riding or noncooperation.*

Human nature makes a distinction between members – be it kin or extended family or tribe – and nonmembers or outsiders who assumedly cannot be trusted. This almost innate tendency resulted in parochial altruism or tribalism whereby our human brains automatically distinguish trustworthy "us" against untrustworthy "them." Humans seem to favor in-group members. Similarly, organizations easily socialize their members into a coherent group of trustworthy individuals – requiring dedicated loyalty in return for organizational "protection." In order to develop the level of cooperation that is necessary for humans to live in large social groups, humans had to become less aggressive and less competitive.[6] From an evolutionary perspective, it is obvious that such a self-domestication process in which overly aggressive or despotic others were either ostracized or killed by the group, helped individuals to cooperate and to survive. Such survival assumes that *free-riders must be punished.* If accountability and responsibility are abolished from the network of such a group or organization, our eco-system may not stand the pressure from selfish short-term players. Reputation is a key to understanding how selflessness can survive beyond the borders of a group, preventing altruists from being exploited and eventually dying out.[7] Voluntary

DOI: 10.1057/9781137547378.0009

sacrifice serves as a signal that a person's intentions are sincere. Altruists can thereby be recognized; their advantage now is that people are willing to trust them. It only requires a consensus about what a society regards as a good deed and thus a sign of *trustworthiness*.

However, market forces and the way we have become used to responding to them give undue weight to competitive advantage while largely ignoring the innovative power of collaboration. Owing to digitization and ICT innovation, that is rapidly changing. Competition between groups and organizations has been the bedrock of modern economics. The current emphasis on competitive forces may not provide a real answer to overcome the tragedy of commons,[8] be it overexploitation of our limited resources, corruptive political forces or harming our environment. An African proverb nicely summarizes it all: "If you want to go quickly, go alone. If you want to go far, go together."

With the increased interdependency and connectivity of globalization and increasingly global systemic and complex challenges, collaborative cocreation between these organizations may become more and more a necessity to find innovative solutions for those challenges, be it an industry answer to increased pollution, climate change, overconsumption, ecological footprint of organizations, energy usage or institutionalized corruption, to just name a few that directly affect businesses. And the digitization of our life world seems to increasingly favor some form of peer collaboration of "commons", as seen in fast growing companies as Zipcar, Airbnb and Uber.

Single-mindedly selfish behavior – the presumed bedrock of business economics behind a veil of an invisible hand to magically hold it all together – usually leads to suboptimal strategies. Indeed, collaborating between corporates remains unnatural to many managers; persistent competition seems to be the answer to improve efficiency and to provide new innovative solutions. Big corporations are open to new innovative ideas, obviously, as long as they are derived from within the organization or entities that seem to resemble them. Unfortunately, managers of those established multinationals are generally not very open to new perspectives if they come from young entrepreneurs. These outsiders who "stay hungry and stay foolish" – to paraphrase Steve Jobs – often create real "expert solutions" much more effectively than complacent executives in established industries.

For example, General Electric's toughest competitors will not be the traditional powerhouses such as Siemens or Schneider Electric, but the

DOI: 10.1057/9781137547378.0009

new tech companies such as Google, Apple, Facebook and Amazon (the extremely powerful 'GAFA' group). The *Internet of Things* and the huge opportunities of *big data analytics* will drastically change the business context and competitive landscape. So what can corporate leadership do to engage creative minds – either within or outside the organization – in this increasingly dynamic and unpredictable business context? Forming partnerships and alliances that encourage a continuous process of relearning,[9] business leaders may like to collaborate with suppliers on new business models, or set up pilot projects that will work only when empathy and trust have been established among the participating cocreators. Once a "reputation" has been formed, scenarios can be suggested that allow integration of envisaged offerings and capabilities to best serve their common goal or customer. Through organizing open innovation challenges, the same GE invited inventive minds worldwide to create more sustainable solutions; it has set up a number of microfactories in the world and by crowdsourcing some cutting-edge ideas for its home appliances business, it was able to move faster from concept to showroom. Because of GE's stellar reputation combined with its willingness to remunerate for great ideas, those inventive entrepreneurs accepted to collaborate and cocreate with GE.

Another option could be to integrate the value chains of different corporations where "one's trash is the other's treasure" and to monetize underutilized assets by sharing them with other companies that need them more. Quite a number of Fortune 500 companies are now embracing industrial symbiosis or "cooperation" that turns waste streams into profit streams. Sharing water, energy and waste materials with other corporate members has helped Michelin, a tyre manufacturer, to reduce its landfill waste by 97 percent, significantly reducing its carbon dioxide impact on the environment.[10]

Corporate leaders may also consider to forge win-win partnerships as in hybrid value chains with civil society and government, creating affordable products and services for the poor. Such initiatives that give big organizations access to profitable new markets while NGOs achieve their desired social impact transcend the traditional corporate social responsibility activities. In this way, GE and Unilever have served millions of the bottom-of-the-pyramid customers. And established companies like Pearson, a leading publishing and education company, has recognized the importance of digital learning tools and online courses; it now partners with promising start-ups, trying to cocreate educational solutions as the Khan Academy did.

DOI: 10.1057/9781137547378.0009

One of the most famous success stories of freely sharing assets is the Android product that through the open-source strategy of Google is now the biggest mobile operating system in the world, having overtaken Apple's iOS. And in June 2014, Elon Musk of Tesla Motors, an electric car manufacturer, decided to give away its core technology to all companies, including Tesla's rivals. Musk, motivated by enlightened self-interest, believes that by opening up Tesla's patent portfolio, the electric cars – counting only for 1 percent of car sales in the United States in 2014 – will become more affordable and cost-effective and, therefore, make a chance to become the industry standard. International companies have most to lose from the prevailing paradigm of *competitive advantage "at all costs."*

Facing enormous economic, ecological and social challenges – all possible real tragedies – corporations, governments and civil society will need to ensure some kind of cooperation on a global scale. Very hard to achieve! The mechanism of reputation may be a good start to help to enhance such global cooperation. Jointly addressing these global challenges may lead to innovative solutions, to be overseen by governmental minimally scripted consensus regulations and carefully watched and followed by NGOs and media. At the end, business is not just about "winning" the competition as in a zero-sum game – that would be misguided – but about "getting better" in a win-win context. And companies can get better by eliminating bureaucracy, empowering employees through self-organization and cultivating a flexible mindset in the workforce. This new frame of mind may see the many resource constraints as a new opportunity to create significantly more business and social value while minimizing the use of diminishing resources such as energy, capital and time.

C.1.3   Caring for "people, planet and profit" in a digitized world versus shareholder value maximization

Empathy is a powerful force behind the ability *to give* and *to care* for others but obviously it is also a source of vulnerability. Corporate reputation is based on the acknowledgement in organizations that relevant stakeholders' concerns – such as pollution, disrespect of human rights, corruption and other social diseases – should not and cannot be ignored. In other words, boards and top executives of such "empathetic" organizations will aim to take decisions that not only optimize shareholder value but also take into account those stakeholders' concerns. However, such an attitude makes them vulnerable for criticism because of apparent contradictory

DOI: 10.1057/9781137547378.0009

statements or actions. It is much easier to focus on maximization of profitability or stockholder value than to optimize investor value while at the same time attempting to resolve some of the stakeholders' or community's concerns. It is in this "good behavior game" that obviously brings benefits to the adherers that we have a glimpse of optimism that corporations, governments and civil organizations may collaborate in a form of evolving solutions to address the challenge of the "commons."

Resolving some of these "commons" will require organizations to embrace the notion of sustainability.[11] There are a number of reasons why organizations should consider to care for "people, planet and profit," to pursue social and environmental goals besides the usual profitability motives:

1 *Business opportunities:* today, sustainability linked to green and ethical products remains a niche market.[12] The numerous bioproducts are proof of that trend. The challenge remains how to incorporate lofty corporate sustainability objectives into the strategy of mainstream companies and translate them in daily operations.

2 *Regulations:* government regulations and industry codes of conduct require that companies increasingly address sustainability. Noncompliance can be costly, be it in terms of penalties and fines, legal costs, lost productivity due to additional inspections and the negative impact on corporate reputation.

3 *Community relations:* identifying the social and environmental issues that are important to key stakeholders and improving relations with them can foster loyalty and trust and provide a society's "license to operate." Moreover, good performance on sustainability can garner a positive reputation with these stakeholders.

4 *Societal and moral obligation:* leadership better shows genuine concern for social and environmental impacts of their organization. That is why organizations recognize and redefine the relationship between business and society around the notion of sustainability. Although there may be no formal "social licensing agreement," society ultimately requires in one form or another that organizations earn their right to operate. When boards and leadership do not consider the impact of their decisions on all stakeholders – not just maximizing shareholders' stock price – they are putting this implicit license to operate at risk that may damage its corporate reputation.

DOI: 10.1057/9781137547378.0009

By emphasizing nonfinancial aspects of business, companies can improve the bottom line and earn superior returns. The Australian BHP-Billiton, the world's largest mining company, focuses on human rights and business ethics that has allowed the company to significantly improve productivity and revenues. Tesla, the electric car, or the Prius, Toyota's hybrid car, are other examples of that increasingly popular environmental niche, capturing new opportunities of the "green movement" in terms of revenues. On the contrary, many companies focus on eco-efficiency to reduce costs or to recycle waste: Enel, Italy's largest utility company, has pledged to half all new investments in coal, decommission fossil-fuel-powered plants in Italy and work towards carbon neutrality by 2050. And there are numerous examples like these: some kind of mindset is shifting to embrace sustainability, either to reduce risks or to capture new opportunities.

By risking their good reputation, selfish CEOs and their organizations seem to create lower return on assets than more virtuous leaders over a longer period. Obviously, if CEOs and boards do not care about their own legacy, and focus only on maximizing their own profitability within the rules of law in the strict sense, then the mechanism of reputation may be a too lenient mechanism to incite these self-focused leadership and boards into more global cooperative behavior. However, research indicates that sustainable companies outperform their peers. One reputable study found a 4.8 percent superior annual abnormal return on investment or stock market performance over the period 1993–2010.[13] Sustainable organizations were also less volatile relative to the portfolio of less sustainable firms. It seems that a number of these environmentally sound and ethical firms are not just idealists but high-performing organizations outmaneuvering their traditional competitors. However, it could just be as well that those green firms are more profitable not because they are green, but because they are better governed and run, explaining the fact that greenness is simply a proxy for good sound management practices.

Moreover, a good board in our opinion *acts like a good housefather –* endorsing the original meaning of *oeconomia –* aiming to create long-term value. Board leadership engages with investors to ensure that all key stakeholders behave in the interest of such continuous sustainable value creation. And good results create a good reputation, allowing trust to unfold. And audible praise for even small contributions to the environmental an ethical good is often more effective than punishing or imposing stringent regulations and rules.

DOI: 10.1057/9781137547378.0009

C.1.4   Governing responsibly beyond compliance versus minimally interpreted fiduciary accountability

Success of getting better[14] involves both capitalizing on the strength of reputational excellence as found in the characteristics of "givers" in organizations and on avoiding the pitfalls of reputational risks of being too selfish that may undermine the group's or organizational survival. That explains why some minimal governance structures – with a fair explicit reward and implicit sanctioning system – could nudge towards more ethical behavior that coordinates actions and prevents exploitation from within.

A board's commitment to sustainability likely will improve the reputation of the organization. It requires boards to focus on (1) steering and providing strategic guidance to ensure a sensible growth and prosperity over a longer period; (2) ensuring accountability and responsibility of the organization to all its key stakeholders, inclusive of investors-owners, employees, customers, suppliers, regulators and community; and (3) guaranteeing that a well-qualified executive team is managing the organization.

A primary goal of board leadership for more sustainability and thus a better corporate reputation is setting principles and practices that will help institutionalize "to become a better corporate citizen." These core governance principles include oversight of top executives, engagement and communication with key stakeholders, alignment of purpose, vision, values and long-term strategy, creation of an open dialogue through diversity and different expertise among board members, ensuring the implementation of accountability and responsibility among all employees and management and evaluating that equitable and fair remuneration system and practices are implemented.

Despite our emphasis on engagement with key stakeholders to take their concerns into account to reduce reputational risks and to enhance reputational excellence, somehow, boards remain ultimately accountable to their shareowners at the annual shareholders' meeting. In order to preserve or to enhance the corporate reputation by continuously creating corporate value, boards may be accounted for (1) pursuing long-term corporate growth strategies; (2) effective transparency and integrity of financial and nonfinancial information; and (3) avoiding company and management misconduct. That may imply "to do good, effectively." And thus, once more, boards may consider polycentric governance as they need to acknowledge many stakes in the organization, not just maximizing share value. Hence why engraining ESG into strategic objectives

DOI: 10.1057/9781137547378.0009

partially mitigates risks since it creates goodwill and trust, which sometimes functions as a safety net against public rage and governmental action when mishaps occur.

The digitization of our society has changed businesses deal with each other. Merely complying does not make an organization or its board a visionary or champion in its field. More than compliance is expected from boards and their organizations. Indeed, the digitization of the global economy has enabled peer-to-peer sharing platforms that have undermined the traditional business models. It is now quite easy for individuals to share their assets, products and skills without the need for intermediaries, and thus dramatically reduce the transaction costs. Growing at 25 percent per annum, the "sharing economy" is expected to grow over USD 100 billion within a few years, without requiring major investments. Airbnb and Uber are the obvious examples. To counter the onslaught by these new tech start-ups, traditional companies like Marriott, world's one of the leading hotel companies, are using the same internet technology – they launched a dedicated website where customers can submit innovate ideas, Travel Brilliantly – to listen to their customers to improve their service. And in such an increasingly interdependent economy, corporate reputation is becoming an universal acceptable "currency."

In other words, global and local companies are focusing more and more on customers' genuine needs. And although boards are still accountable for monitoring their top executive team and for the performance of the company, corporate leadership has been waken up by this technology revolution, which is hugely changing the business landscape. Acting wisely implies that boards will take a slightly more active role in coaching and guiding top executives to make the right choices and act more responsibly in this dynamic and ever more transparent business context. It also means that boards will need to make time for discussing strategic choices that go well beyond just signing off on the appropriateness of the disclosure of the company's financial data, their traditional fiduciary function. Successful and visionary boards are learning fast to steer their organization toward long-term strategic value creation.

C.2   The vulnerability of reputation, based on trust

What is more important for survival in the business world? Truth (about a certain product or service) or corporate reputation? Whether we like it

DOI: 10.1057/9781137547378.0009

or not, appearance is usually far more important than reality. However, our brains are programmed to be looking constantly for checking the reputation of others, to question the trustworthiness of others.[15] And on top of that the digitization of our world has forced more transparency upon us. It is therefore highly recommendable that leadership and their organizations behave in a trustworthy manner. By consistently acting according to desired characteristics of what the company's identity stands for, the organization may convince its stakeholders that it is worth their trust. Humans progress by trusting others beyond the purely rational rule of looking out only for oneself. The expectation is that this generous act of trust will later be reciprocated by the other who has obtained a reputation to be trustworthy. It is not the ruthless pursuit of selfish maximization of profitability that makes a society prosperous, but it is the accumulation of trust that allows members to cooperate and enhance their wealth. People like John Huntsman Senior[16] became so successful in business because he was a "giver," always there to help others, being committed to give back where possible.[17] It is that reputation that made him a very trustworthy and reliable man whom people wanted to do business with. Moreover, national economies in which individuals believe one another to be generous or trustworthy do grow faster than others.[18]

However, this act of trusting incurs the risk of *vulnerability* that the other may take advantage of such "cooperative" (sometimes generous) behavior. This vulnerability is somehow alleviated by the expectation of reciprocity. Thus if all goes well, a virtuous spiral of trust is created.[19] Because trusting others gives rise to *vulnerability*, anything that provides grounds for mutual assurance helps reduce that perceived vulnerability. A good reputation can often generate significant new business, while a bad reputation can sink the firm's efforts to grow. A 'safe' place[20] needs to be created that invites deep listening and vulnerability – the necessary ingredients for inner truth to emerge. Though it may seem counterintuitive, vulnerability and strength are not in opposition but rather mutually reinforcing polarities.

This *paradox of trust* tells us that we are better off in pursuing our own interests by laying them aside and serving others. When corporate leadership is willing to give up the desire to be in full control, it will gain cooperation and trust, and thus indirectly more "control" over the ultimate corporate objectives. In the same vein of thinking, we believe that organizations would be better off in the long term if pure profit maximization were replaced by a more enlightened way of managing limited

DOI: 10.1057/9781137547378.0009

resources and sharing some of the benefits that the organization creates with other involved stakeholders. Anyone who has ever negotiated with suppliers in a global supply chain knows the benefits of having a good reputation and of treating a business partner in a fair way, especially if the aim is a long collaboration. The strength of good reputation enhances reciprocal benevolent cooperative behavior. Nevertheless, the rewards of cooperation are often supported by a mechanism of (potential) punishment for defecting. Indeed, companies that are able to retaliate for undermining a collaborative agreement can use this deterrent. And where such potential retaliation works, the punishment is paradoxically hardly necessary.[21]

Excellence or greatness through mastery, autonomous self-esteem and meaningful purpose does not seem to be fully compatible with myopic short-termism. Wise and resilient leadership built on appropriate foundations of good corporate governance may have a better chance to lift one's sight and push toward longer-term horizons.

We may have a glimmer hope that some solutions for these global challenges can be achieved when leadership acknowledges the *shadow of one's own future*. Broadening one's horizon of concern beyond the events of tomorrow will help to extend the shadow of one's future. And caring for reputational excellence – despite its incredible inherent *vulnerability* – may possibly help on that journey to overcome the human tragedy of commons. And having created a legacy could be a worthy reputational side effect.

Enhancing corporate reputational excellence may help to nudge corporate behavior to embrace nonfinancial objectives that may give more meaning to its corporate activities, inciting leaders and their organizations to regain some balance. Leadership and governing an organization is about serving others, even willing to sacrifice. That attitude of good leadership as in an enlightened fiduciary duty of loyalty and care creates trust, the belief that this leadership has the well-being of their employees, customers, investors and key stakeholders at heart. However, trust is granted to either an organization or its leadership and therefore corporate reputation will always remain vulnerable.

Notes

1   Williams, Schnake & Fredenberger 2005.
2   See Chapter 1.

3   Kanter 2011.
4   Kramer 2010.
5   Blood 2015.
6   Gazzaniga 2011.
7   Klein 2014.
8   See Chapter 2.
9   Radjou & Prabhu 2015.
10 Radjou & Prabhu 2015: 160.
11 Epstein 2008: 36–37. The nine principles of sustainability performance could be described as following:

> (1) Ethics: the company establishes, promotes, monitors, and maintains ethical standards ad practices in dealings with all of the company stakeholders; (2) Governance: the company manages all of its resources conscientiously and effectively, recognizing the fiduciary duty of corporate boards and managers to focus on the interests of all company stakeholders; (3) Transparency: the company provides timely disclosure of information about its products, services, and activities, thus permitting stakeholders to make informed decisions; (4) Business relationships: the company engages in fair-trading practices with suppliers, distributors, and partners; (5) Financial return: the company compensates providers of capital with a competitive return on investment and the protection of company assets; (6) Community involvement/economic development: the company fosters a mutually beneficial relationship between the corporation and community in which it is sensitive to the culture, context, and needs of the community; (7) Value of products and services: the company respects the needs, desires, and rights of its customers and strives to provide the highest level of product and service values; (8) the company engages in human-resource management practices that promote personal and professional employee development, diversity and empowerment; and (9) Protection of the environment: the company strives to protect and restore the environment and promote sustainable development with products, processes, services and other activities.

12 Vogel 2005.
13 Eccles, Ioannou & Serafeim 2011.
14 This is paraphrasing the intriguing article by Holly Schroth (2011): "it is not about winning, it's about getting better."
15 Klein 2014; Pfaff 2015.
16 Jon Huntsman Senior is a friend of my business partner and friend Paul Morse who speaks highly of him. However, Huntsman's reputation has traveled much further and it seems that most people who have met Mr. Huntsman have developed a likening of him because of his genuine and authentic generosity.
17 Grant 2013: 182. In his "memoirs" *Winners Never Cheat,* Huntsman Senior writes that "Monetarily, the most satisfying moments in my life have not been the excitement of closing a great deal or the reaping of profits from it. They have been when I was able to help others in need...There is no denying that I am a deal junkie, but I also have developed an addiction for giving.

DOI: 10.1057/9781137547378.0009

The more one gives, the better one feels; and the better one feels about it, the easier it becomes to give." We agree with professor Grant's conclusion – based on empirical research – that giving can boost happiness and meaning, motivating people to work harder and earn more money. In the same line of thinking one can easily stipulate or corroborate that meaning is associated with being a "giver" more than a selfish taker. And yes, by giving in ways that give meaning and provide the energy to continue to do so, rather than being exhausted by "vampire-like" manipulators, these otherish givers (i.e., a conditional giver who shares but will attempt to protect against being manipulated or exhaustively drained) – a term quipped by Adam Grant – are more likely to rise to the top. Apparently, successful givers are able to distinguish those who are likely to manipulate them from people genuinely in need. That critical distinction of spotting real trustworthy people protects givers from manipulation.

18   Knack & Keefer 1997. Assume that 7 percent more citizens agree with the statement that one can trust most people, it translates into a 1 percent increase in annual economic growth.

19   Klein 2014: 48–50. Trust in others seems to be a product of elemental functions of the brain to which human beings owe their own survival in Darwinian terms. It also means that a functioning, mutually beneficial relationship is by no means merely the result of rational choices. No, it rests on an emotional foundation.

20   Verhezen 2015, Laloux 2014. Being respectfully and compassionately "held" by a group in an organization is for many people a new and unforgettable experience.

21   Unfortunately, the opposite is also true. Corruption and tax cheating can spread in a society like infectious cancer. Without control or punishment, and in the absence of a big number of responsible managers or public officials, corruption will prevail. The morality of a group relies on the mechanism of trust and reputation; without these, cooperation (to curb corruption) collapses.

DOI: 10.1057/9781137547378.0009

References

Abraham, S.E., (2008), "Is publication of the reputation quotient (RQ) sufficient to move stock prices?", *Corporate Reputation Review*, Vol. 11 (4): 308–319.

Adams, J.E.; S. Highhouse & M.J. Zickar, (2010), "Understanding general distrust of corporations", *Corporate Reputation Review*, Vol. 13 (1): 38–51.

Admati, A. & M. Hellwig, (2013), *The bankers' new clothes. What's wrong with banking and what to do about it*, Princeton; Oxford, Princeton University Press.

Alsop, R.J., (2006), *The 18 immutable laws of corporate reputation. Creating, protecting & repairing your most valuable asset*, London, Kogan Page Books.

Ang, S.H. & A.M. Wight, (2009), "Building intangible resources: the stickiness of reputation", *Corporate Reputation Review*, Vol. 12 (1): 21–32.

Argenti, P.A. & G. Aarons, (2011), "Digital strategies for enhancing reputation", in A. Hiles (Ed), *Reputation management. Building and protecting your company's profile in a digital world*, London, Bloomsbury, pp.115–126.

Axelrod, R., (1984), *The evolution of cooperation*, New York, Basic Books.

Axelrod, R. & W.D. Hamilton, (1981), "The evolution of cooperation", *Science*, Vol. 211: 1390–1396.

Baier, A.C., (1994), *Moral prejudices. Essays on ethics*, Cambridge MA, Harvard University Press.

Barnett, M.L; J.M. Jermier & B.A. Lafferty, (2006), "Corporate reputation: the definitional landscape", *Corporate Reputation Review*, Vol. 9 (1): 26–38.

Baron, D.P., (2011), "Goldman Sachs and its Reputation", Stanford Graduate School of Business Case, Distributed by the Case Centre, p.77.

Barton, D. & M. Wiseman, (2015), "Focusing capital on the long term", in J.G. Taft (Ed), *A force for good. How enlightened finance can restore faith in capitalism*, New York, Palgrave Macmillan, pp.215–230.

Bazerman, M.H., (2014), "Becoming a first-class noticer. How to spot and prevent ethical failures in your organization", *Harvard Business Review*, July–August: 116–119.

Bazerman, M.H. & A.E. Tenbrunsel, (2011), "Ethical breakdowns", *Harvard Business Review*, April: 58–65.

Benabou, R. & J. Tirole, (2003), "Intrinsic and extrinsic motivation", *Review of Economic Studies*, Vol. 70: 503–504.

Bennedsen, M., (2013), "East meets West. Rothschild's Investment in Indonesia's Bakrie Group", *INSEAD Case*, 12/2013-6030; INS301.

Berger, I.; P. Cunningham & M. Drumwright, (2007), "Mainstreaming corporate social responsibility: developing markets for virtue", *California Management Review*, Summer, Vol. 49 (4): 132–156.

Bierly, P.; E. Kessler & E. Christensen, (2000), "Organizational learning knowledge and wisdom", *Journal of Organizational Change*, Vol. 13 (6): 595–618.

Birkinshaw, J.; N.J. Foss & S. Lindenberg, (2014), "Combining purpose with profits", *MIT Sloan Management Review*, Spring: 48–56.

Blood, D., (2015), "Sustainable capitalism", in J.G. Taft, *A force for good. How enlightened finance can restore faith in capitalism*, New York, Palgrave Macmillan, pp.231–242.

Bogle, J.C., (2015), "The fiduciary principle: no man can serve two masters", in J.G. Taft (Ed), *A force for good. How enlightened finance can restore faith in capitalism*, New York, Palgrave Macmillan, pp.81–90.

Bonini, S.; D. Court & A. Marchi, (2009), "Rebuilding corporate reputations", *The McKinsey Quarterly*, June, pp.1–8.

Bonini, S.; T.M. Koller & P.H. Mirvis, (2009), "Valuing social responsibility programs", *Business in Society*, Vol. 4: 65–73.

Bose, I. & N. Celly, (2011), "The Indian tiger prowls in Africa: Bharti Airtel's acqiusition of Zain Africa", *Asia Case Research Centre*, Hong Kong University.

Brandenburger, A.M. & B.J. Nalebuff, (1996), *Co-opetition*, New York, Currency Doubleday.

DOI: 10.1057/9781137547378.0010

Bromley, D.; (2002), "Comparing corporate reputations: league tables, quotients, benchmarks, or case studies?", *Corporate Reputation Review*, Vol. 5 (1): 35–50.

Camerer, C.F. & E. Feher, (2006), "When does 'economic man' dominate social behavior?", *Science*, Vol. 311: 47–52.

Cassimon, D.; P-J. Engelen; L. Van Liedekerke & P. Verhezen, (2007), "Investing in corporate social reputation: a real option approach", nonpublished paper, presented at EBEN Conference, Leuven, April 2007.

Chaher, S. & J.D. Spellman, (2012), "Corporate governance and social media: a brave new world for board directors", IFC World Bank Website, A Global Corporate Governance Forum Publication. Private Sector Opinion Issue No 27.

Charan, R., (2013), *Global tilt. Leading your business through the great economic power shift*, New York, Random House.

Charan, R., (2015), *The attacker's advantage. Turning uncertainty into breakthrough opportunities*, New York, Public Affairs.

Charan, R.; D. Carey & M. Useem, (2014), *Boards that lead. When to take charge, when to partner, and when to stay out the way*, Cambridge MA, Harvard Business School Press.

Chin-Shin, L., (2010), "The effects of CSR on Brand Performance's mediating effect of corporate reputation", *Journal of Business Ethics*, Vol. 95(3): 457–469.

Christensen, C.M., (1997), *Disruptive innovation*, Cambridge MA, Harvard Business School Press.

Christensen, C.M.; J. Allworth & K. Dillon, (2012), *How will you measure life? Finding fulfilment using lessons from some of the world's greatest businesses*, London, HarperCollins.

Collins, J., (2001), *From good to great: why some companies make the leap...and others don't*, New York, Harper Business.

Collins, J., (2009), *How the mighty fall. And why some companies never give in*, New York, HarperCollins.

Conference Board USA, (2010), *Reputation risk. A corporate governance perspective*, ISBN No. 0-8237-0906-X.

Courtney, H., (2001), "Making the most of uncertainty", *The MCKinsey Quarterly*, (4): 38–47.

Courtright, J.L. & P.M. Smudde, (2009), "Leveraging oganizational innovation for strategic reputation management", *Corporate Reputation Review*, Vol. 12 (3): 245–269.

DOI: 10.1057/9781137547378.0010

Davies, Gary with R. Chun; R. Vinhas da Solva & S. Roper, (2003), *Corporate reputation and competitiveness*, London; New York, Routledge Publications.

Dawkins, R., (1976 [1989]), *The selfish gene*, Oxford, Oxford University Press.

De Castro, G.M.; J. Lopez & P. L. Saez, (2006), "Business and social reputation: exploring the concept and main dimensions of corporate reputation", *Journal of Business Ethics*, (63): 361–370.

De Quevedo-Puente, E.; De la Fuente-Sabate & J. B. Delgado-Garcia, (2007), "Corporate social performance and corporate reputation: two interwoven perspectives", *Corporate Reputation Review*, Vol. 10 (1): 60–72.

Del Vecchio, P.; R. Laubacher; V. Ndou & G. Passiante, (2011), "Managing corporate reputation in the blogosphere: the case of DELL computer", *Corporate Reputation Review*, Vol. 14 (2): 133–144.

Deephouse, D., (2002), "The term 'reputation management': users, uses and trademark tradeoff", *Corporate Reputation Review*, Vol. 5 (1): 9–18.

Deloitte, (2011), *Board practices report*: 17 practices report: Design, Composition and Function.

Diermeier, D., (2011), *Reputation rules. Strategies for building your company's most valuable asset*, New York, McGrawHill.

Dimma, W., (2002), *Excellence in the boardroom. Best practices in corporate directorship*, Ontario, Wiley & Sons Canada.

Divol, R.; D. Edelman & H. Saarzin, (2012), "Demystifying social media", *McKinsey Quarterly*, April, http://www.mckinseyonmarketingandsales.com/demystifying-social-media-2.

Dixit, A.K. & B.J. Nalebuff, (2010), *The art of strategy. A game theorist's guide to success in business and life*, New York; London, W.W. Norton.

Dowdell, T.; S. Govindaraj & P. Jain, (1992), "The Tylenol incident, ensuing regulation and stock prices", *The Journal of Financial and Quantitative Analysis*, Vol. 27 (2): 283–301.

Dowling, G.R., (2006a), "Communicating corporate reputation through stories", *California Management Review*, Vol. 49 (1): 82–100.

Dowling, G.R., (2006b), "How good corporate reputation create corporate value", *Corporate Reputation Review*, Vol. 9 (2): 134–143.

Dowling, G.R., (2006c), "In practice: how good corporate reputations create corporate value", *Corporate Reputation Review*, Vol. 9 (2): 134–143.

Dowling, G.R. & W. Weeks, (2008), "What the media is really telling you about your brand", *MIT Sloan Management Review*, Spring, Vol. 49 (3): 27–34.

Eccles, R.G. & G. Serafeim, (2013), "The performance frontier. Innovating for a sustainable strategy", *Harvard Business Review*, November: 50–60.

DOI: 10.1057/9781137547378.0010

Eccles, R.G.; I. Ioannou & G. Serafeim, (2011), "The impact of a corporate culture of sustainability on corporate behavior and performance", Working Paper, Harvard Business School.

Eccles, R.G.; S.C. Newquist & R. Schatz, (2007), "Reputation and its risks", *Harvard Business Review*, February: 104–114.

Eisenbeiss, S.A. & F. Brodbeck, (2014), "Ethical and unethical leadership: a cross-cultural and cross-sectoral analysis", *Journal of Business Ethics*, Vol. 122: 343–359.

Eisenstat, R.A.; M. Beer; N. Foote; T. Fredberg & F. Norrgren, (2008), "The uncompromising leader", *Harvard Business Review*, July–August: 51–57.

Elkington, J., (1997), *Cannibals with forks: The triple bottom line of 21st century business*, Oxford, Capstone.

Elkington, J. & J. Zeitz, (2015), *The breakthrough challenge. 10 ways to connect today's profits with tomorrow's bottom line*, San Francisco, Jossey Bass.

Emerson, J., (2003), "The blended value proposition: integrating social and financial returns", *California Management Review*, Vol. 45 (4): 35–51.

Epstein, M., (2008), *Making sustainability work. Best practices in managing and measuring corporate social, environmental, and economic impacts*, San Francisco, Berrett-Koehler Publishers-Greenleaf Publishing.

Erhard, W.H. & M.C. Jensen, (2011), "The three foundations of a great life, great leadership, and a great organization", *Harvard NOM Unit Research Paper,* No. 11–12.

Erhard, W.H.; M.C. Jensen & S. Zaffron, (2010), "Integrity: a positive model that incorporates the normative phenomena of morality, ethics, and legality", *Harvard Business School Working Paper*, March.

Ettenson, R. & J. Knowles, (2008), "Don't confuse reputation with brand", *MIT Sloan Management Review*, Vol. 49 (2): 18–21.

Fehr, E., (2015a), "Altruistic punishment and creation of public goods", in T. Singer & M. Ricard (Eds), *Caring economics*, New York, Picador, pp.125–134.

Fehr, E., (2015b), "The social dilemma experiment", in T. Singer & M. Ricard (Eds), *Caring economics*, New York, Picador, pp.77–84.

Fehr, E. & S. Gaechter, (2002), "Altruistic punishment in humans", *Nature*, Vol. 415: 137–40.

Fertik, M. & D. Thompson, (2015), *Reputation economy. How to optimize your digital footprint in a world here your reputation is your most valuable asset*, New York, Crown Business (Random House).

Firestein, P., (2009), *Crisis of character. Building corporate reputation in the age of skepticism*, New York, Sterling Publishing.

DOI: 10.1057/9781137547378.0010

Fombrun, C.J., (1996), *Reputation: realizing value from the corporate image*, Cambridge, Harvard Business School Press.

Fombrun, C.J., (2006a), "Corporate governance", *Corporate Reputation Review*, Vol. 8 (4): 267–271.

Fombrun, C.J., (2006b), "Corporate reputations in China: how do consumers feel about companies?", *Corporate Reputation Review*, Vol. 9 (3): 165–170.

Fombrun, C.J., (2007), "List of lists: a compilation of international corporate reputation ratings", *Corporate Reputation Review*, Vol. 10 (2): 144–153.

Fombrun, C.J. & C. Van Riel, (1997), "The reputation landscape", *Corporate Reputation Review*, Vol. 1: 5–13.

Fombrun, C.J. & M. Pan, (2006), "Corporate reputations in China: how to consumers feel about companies?", *Corporate Reputation Review*, Vol. 9 (3): 165–170.

Fombrun, C.J. & M. Shanley (1990), "What's in the name? Reputation building and corporate strategy", *Academy of Management Review*, Vol. 33 (2): 233–258.

Fombrun, C.; N. Gardberg & J. Sever, (2000), "The reputation quotient: a multi-stakeholder measure of corporate reputation", *Journal of Brand Management*, Vol. 7 (4): 241–255.

Frank, R.H., (1988), *Passions within reason: the strategic role of emotions*, New York, W.W. Norton.

Freeman, R.E., (1984), *Strategic management: a stakeholder approach*, Boston, Pitman.

Freeman, R.E. (Ed), (2010), *Stakeholder theory*, Cambridge, Cambridge University Press.

Freeman, R.E.; L. Dunham & J. McVea, (2007), "Strategic ethics – strategy, wisdom, and stakeholder theory: a pragmatic and entrepreneurial view of stakeholder strategy", in E.H. Kessler & J.R. Bailey (Eds), *Handbook of organizational and managerial wisdom*, Los Angeles; London, Sage Publications, pp.151–180.

Frey, B., (1997), *Not just for the money – an economic theory of personal motivation*, Cheltentam UK, Edward Elgar.

Friedman, M., (1970), "The social responsibility of business is to increase its profits", *New York Times Magazine*, September 13: 32–33, 122, 126.

Gardberg, N.A., (2006), "Reputatie, reputation, réputation, reputazione, ruf: a cross-cultural qualitative analysis of construct and instrument equivalence", *Corporate Reputation Review*, Vol. 9 (1): 39–61.

Gardner, H.K., (2015), "When senior managers won't collaborate", *Harvard Business Review*, March: 75–82.

DOI: 10.1057/9781137547378.0010

Gazzaniga, M., (2011), *Who's in charge? Free will and the science of the brain*, New York, HarperCollins.

Gentile, M.C., (2010), "Keeping your colleagues honest", *Harvard Business Review*, March: 114–117.

George, B. & J.W. Lorsch, (2014), "How to outsmart activist investors?", *Harvard Business Review*, May: 89–95.

Geppert, J. & J.E. Lawrence, (2008), "Predicting firm reputation through content analysis of shareholders' letter", *Corporate Reputation Review*, Vol. 11 (4): 285–307.

Govier, T., (1998), *Dilemmas of trust*, Montreal; London, McGill Queens University.

Granovetter, M., (1983), "The strength of weak ties: a network theory revisited", *Sociological Theory*, Vol. 1: 201–233.

Grant, A., (2013), *Give and take. Why helping others drives our success,* New York, Penguin.

Gratton, L., (2011), *The shift. The future of work is already here*, London, William Collins (Harper Collins).

Gratton, L., (2014), *The key. How corporations succeeded by solving the world's toughest problems*, New York, McGrawHill.

Green, J., (2013), *Moral tribes. Emotion, reason and the gap between us and them*, London, Atlantic Books (Penguin).

Green, S., (2009), *Good value. Reflections on money, morality and an uncertain world*, London, Allen Lane.

Haidt, J., (2012), *The righteous mind. Why good people are divided by politics and religion*, New York, Vintage Books.

Hall, S.S., (2010), *Wisdom. From philosophy to neuroscience*, St Lucia, University of Queensland Press.

Handy, Ch., (2015), *The Second Curve. Thoughts on Reinventing Society*, London, Random House.

Hansen, M.T.; H. Ibarra & U. Peyer, (2013), "The best performing CEOs in the world", *Harvard Business Review*, January–February: 81–95.

Hanson, R., (2011), "Life After NPS. Controversy still surrounds the use of net promoter score", *Marketing Research*, Summer: 8–11.

Hardin, G., (1968), "The tragedy of the commons", *Science*, pp.1243–1248.

Harrison, J.S. & A.C. Wicks, (2013), "Stakeholder theory, value and firm performance", *Business Ethics Quarterly*, Vol. 23 (1): 97–124.

Helm, S., (2005), "Designing a formative measure for corporate reputation", *Corporate Reputation Review*, Vol. 8 (2): 95–109.

Helm, S., (2007), "The role of corporate reputation in determining investor satisfaction and loyalty", *Corporate Reputation Review*, Vol. 10 (1): 22–37.

DOI: 10.1057/9781137547378.0010

Henderson, R., (2015). Making the business case for environmental sustainability. *Harvard Business School Working Paper* 15-068, February.

Hiles, A. (Ed), (2011), *Reputation management. Building and protecting your company's profile in a digital world*, London, Bloomsbury.

Hill, L.A.; G. Brandeau; E. Truelove & K. Lineback, (2014), "Collective genius", *Harvard Business Review*, Jan: 94–102.

Hunter, M.L.; M. Le Menestrel & H-Cl de Bettignies, (2008), "Beyond control: crisis strategies and stakeholder media in the Danone boycott of 2001", *Corporate Reputation Review*, Vol. 11 (4): 335–350.

Isaacson, W., (2014), *Innovators*, New York, Simon & Schuster.

Jackson, K.T., (2004), *Building reputational capital. Strategies for integrity and fair play that improve the bottom line*, Oxford, Oxford University Press.

Jackson, Ira A. & Jane Nelson, (2004), *Profits with principles. Seven strategies delivering value with values*, New York, Currency Doubleday.

Jensen, M., (1986), "Agency cost of free cash flow, corporate finance, and takeovers", *American Economic Review*, Vol. 76 (2): 323–329.

Jensen, M., (2002), "Value maximization, stakeholder theory, and the corporate objective function", *Business Ethics Quarterly*, Vol. 12 (2): 235–256.

Jensen, M. & W.H. Meckling, (1976), "Theory of the firm: managerial behavior, agency costs and ownership structure", *Journal of Financial Economics*, reprinted in Th. Clarke (Ed), 2004, *Theories of corporate governance. The philosophical foundations of corporate governance*, London, Routledge, pp.58–63.

Jones, C.A., (2005), "Wisdom paradigms for the enhancement of ethical and profitable business practices", *Journal of Business Ethics*, Vol. 57: 363–375.

Kanter, R. Moss, (2011), "How great companies think differently", *Harvard Business Review*, November: 66–78.

Kaplan, R.S. & A. Mikes, (2012), "Managing risks. A new framework", *Harvard Business Review*, June: 48–60.

Kiel, F., (2015), *Return on character. The real reason leaders and their companies win*, Cambridge MA, Harvard Business School Press.

Kim, S., (2014), "What's worse in terms of product-harm crisis? Negative corporate ability or negative corporate social responsibility?", *Journal of Business Ethics*, Vol. 123 (1): 157–170.

Kim, W.C. & R. Mauborgne, (2014), "Blue ocean leadership", *Harvard Business Review*, May: 60–72.

King, B.G. & D.A. Whetten, (2008), "Rethinking the relationship between reputation and legitimacy: a social actor conceptualization", *Corporate Reputation Review*, Vol. 11 (3): 192–207.

DOI: 10.1057/9781137547378.0010

Klein, S., (2014), *Survival of the nicest. How altruism made us human, and why it pays to get along*, Brunswick Vic, Scribe Publications.

Klewes, J. & R. Wreschniok, (2011), "Smart use of reputation capital: how to benefit from different reputation investment strategies", in A. Hiles (Ed), *Reputation management. Building and protecting your company's profile in a digital world*, London, Bloomsbury, pp.45–57.

Knack, S. & P. Keefer, (1997), "Does social capital have an economic payoff? A cross-cultural investigation", *Quarterly Journal of Economics*, Vol. 112 (4): 1251–1288.

Korten, D.C., (2015), *Change the story, change the future. A living economy for a living earth*, Oakland CA, Berrett-Koehler.

Kramer, R.M., (2009), "Rethinking trust", *Harvard Business Review*, June: 69–77.

Kramer, R.M., (2010), "Collective trust within organizations: conceptual foundations and empirical insights", *Corporate Reputation Review*, Vol. 13 (2): 82–96.

Laloux, F., (2014), *Reinventing organizations. A guide to creating organizations inspired by the next stage of human consciousness*, Brussels, Nelson Parker.

Larkin, J., (2003), *Strategic reputation risk management*, New York, Palgrave Macmillan.

Lazonick, W., (2014), "Profits without prosperity", *Harvard Business Review*, September: 42–55.

Lee, M-Y; A. Fairhurst & S. Wesley, (2009), "Corporate social responsibility: a review of the top 100 US retailers", *Corporate Reputation Review*, Vol. 12 (2): 140–158.

Lehrer, M. & C. Delaunay, (2009), "Multinational enterprises and the promotion of civil society: the challenge for 21st century capitalism", *California Management Review*, Vol. 51 (4): 126–147.

Lev, B., (2012), *Winning investors over*, Cambridge MA, Harvard Business Review Press.

Lindgreen, A. & V. Swaen, (2010), "Corporate social responsibility", *International Journal of Management Review*, Vol. 10: 1–7.

Lindgreen, A.; V. Swaen & F. Maon, (2009), "CSR with the organization", *Corporate Reputation Review*, Vol. 12 (2): 83–86.

Livingston, J.A., (2005), "How valuable is a good reputation? A sample selection model of internet auctions", *The Review of Economics and Statistics*, Vol. 87 (3): 453–465.

DOI: 10.1057/9781137547378.0010

Loo, T. & G. Davies, (2006), "Branding China: the ultimate challenge in reputation management", *Corporate Reputation Review*, Vol. 9 (3): 198–210.

Lorsch, J.W. & R.C. Clark, (2008), "Leading from the boardroom", *Harvard Business Review*, April, pp.104–111.

Macey, J.R., (2008), *Corporate governance. Promises kept, promises broken*, New Jersey, Princeton University Press.

Macey, J.R., (2013), *The death of corporate reputation. How integrity has been destroyed on Wall Street*, New Jersey, Pearson Education FT Press.

Mackey, J., (2011), "What conscious capitalism really is", *California Management Review*, Spring, Vol. 53 (3): 83–90.

Mackey, J. & R. Sisodia, (2013), *Conscious capitalism. Liberating the heroic spirit of business*, Cambridge MA, Harvard Business Review Press.

Madsen, P. & J.M. Shafritz (Eds), (1990), *Essentials of Business Ethics*, New York, Penguin Books.

Margolis, J.D. & J.P. Walsh, (2001), "Does it pay to be good? An analysis and redirection of research on the relationship between corporate social and financial performance", Working Paper, Harvard University.

Margolis, J.D. & J.P. Walsh, (2003), "Misery loves companies: social initiatives by business", *Administrative Science Quarterly*, 48: 268–305.

Marquis, C. & M.W. Toffel, (2011), "The globalization of corporate environmental disclosure: accountability or greenwashing?", *Harvard Business Review Working Papers*, 11–115.

McCann, J. & M. Sweet, (2014), "The perceptions of ethical and sustainable leadership", *Journal of Business Ethics*, Vol. 121: 373–383.

McKenna, B.; D. Rooney & K.B. Boal, (2009), "Wisdom principles as a meta-theoretical basis for evaluating leadership", *The Leadership Quarterly*, Vol. 20: 177–190.

McLaughlin, K. & D. McMillon, (2015), "Business and society in the coming decades", *McKinsey & Company*, April.

McWilliams, A.; D.S. Siegel & P.M. Wright, (2006), "Corporate social responsibility: strategic implications", *Journal of Management Studies*, Vol. 43 (1): 1–18.

Meyer, C. & J. Kirby, (2010), "Leadership in the age of transparency", *Harvard Business Review*, April, pp.38–46.

Michelon, G., (2011), "Sustainability disclosure and reputation: a comparative study", *Corporate Reputation Review*, Vol. 14 (1): 79–96.

Milinski, M.; D. Semmann & H.J. Krambeck, (2002), "Reputation helps solve the tragedy of commons", *Nature*, Vol. 415: 424–26.

DOI: 10.1057/9781137547378.0010

Milne, M.J. & R. Gray, (2013), "W(h)ither ecology? The triple bottom line, the global reporting initiative, and corporate sustainability reporting", *Journal of Business Ethics*, Vol. 118: 13–29.

Minor, D. & J. Morgan, (2011), "CSR as reputation insurance: primum non-nocere", *California Management Review*, Spring, Vol. 53 (3): 40–59.

Mintzberg, H., (1983), "The case for corporate social responsibility", *Journal of Business Strategy*, Vol. 4, pp 3–15.

Mishra, S. & S.B. Modi, (2013), "Positive and negative corporate social responsibility, financial leverage, and idiosyncratic risk", *Journal of Business Ethics*, Vol. 117: 431–448.

Monks, R.; A. Miller & J. Cook, (2004), "Shareholder activism on environmental issues: a study of proposals at large US corporations (2000–2003)", *Natural Resources Forum*, Vol. 28: 317–330.

Neef, D., (2005), "Managing corporate reputation and risk", *Corporate Reputation Review*, Vol. 8 (2): 164–168.

Nobel, C., (2015), *Need to solve a problem? Take a break from collaborating*, Harvard Business School Working Knowledge, Research & Ideas, 4 May.

Nowak, M.A., (1993), "A strategy of win-stay, lose-shift that outperforms tit-for-tat in prisoner's dilemma", *Nature*, Vol. 364: 56–58.

Nowak, M.A., (1998), "Evolution of indirect reciprocity by image scoring", *Nature*, Vol. 393: 573–577.

Nowak, M.A., (2004), "Evolution of indirect reciprocity", *Nature*, Vol. 437: 1291–1298.

Nowak, M.A., (2006a), *Evolutionary dynamics. Exploring the equations of life*. Cambridge MA; London, Belknap Press of Harvard University.

Nowak, M.A., (2006b), "Five rules for the evolution of cooperation", *Science*, December, Vol. 314: 1560–1563.

Nowak, M.A., (2013), "Five rules for the evolution of cooperation", in M.A. Nowak & S. Coakley (Eds), (2013), *Evolution, games and god. The principle of cooperation*, Cambridge MA, Harvard University Press, pp.99–114.

Nowak, M.A. & K. Sigmund, (1992), "Tit for tat in heterogeneous populations", *Nature*, Vol. 355: 250–253.

Nowak, M.A. & K. Sigmund, (1993), "A strategy of win-stay, lose-shift that outperforms tit-for-tat in the prisoner's dilemma", *Nature*, Vol. 364: 56–58.

Nowak, M.A. & K. Sigmund, (1998), "Evolution of indirect reciprocity by image scoring", *Nature*, Vol. 393: 573–577.

Nowak, M.A. & K. Sigmund, (2005), "Evolution of indirect reciprocity", *Nature*, Vol. 437: 1291–1298.

DOI: 10.1057/9781137547378.0010

Nowak, M.A. & S. Coakley (Eds), (2013), *Evolution, games and god. The principle of cooperation*, Cambridge MA, Harvard University Press.

Novak, M.A. with R. Highfield, (2011), *Supercooperators. Altruism, evolution, and why we need each other to succeed*, New York; London, Free Press.

Obloj, T. & K. Obloj, (2006), "Diminishing returns from reputation: do followers have a competitive advantage", *Corporate Reputation Review*, Vol. 9 (4): 213–224.

Olanrewaju, T.; K. Smaje & P. Willmott, (2014), "The seven traits of effective digital enterprises", *McKinsey & Company*, May.

Orlitzky, M., (2011), "Institutional logics in the study of organizations: the social construction of the relationship between corporate social and financial performance", *Business Ethics Quarterly*, Vol. 21 (3): 409–444.

Orlitzky, M.; D.S. Siegel & D.A. Waldman, (2011), "Strategic corporate social responsibility and environmental sustainability", *Business & Society*, Vol. 50 (1): 6–27.

Osterloh, M. & B.S. Frey, (2004), "Corporate governance for crooks? The case for corporate virtue", in A. Grandori (Ed), *Corporate governance and firm organization*, Oxford, Oxford University Press.

Ostrom, E., (1990), *Governing the commons: the evolution of institutions for collective action*. Cambridge, Cambridge University Press.

Ostrom, E., (2010), "Beyond markets and states: polycentric governance of complex economic systems", *American Economic Review*, Vol. 100: 1–33.

Paine, L.S., (1994), "Managing for organizational integrity", *Harvard Business Review*, Boston MA, Vol. 72: 106–117.

Paine, L.S., (2003), *Values shift*, New York, McGraw Hill, p.302.

Pauli, G., (2012), *Blauwe Economie. 10 jaar,100 innovaties, 100 miljoen banen*, Amsterdam, Uitg Nieuw Amsterdam.

Pentland, A., (2008), *Honest signals. How they shape our world*, Cambridge MA, MIT Paperback Press.

Pentland, A., (2013), "Beyond the echo chamber", *Harvard Business Review*, November: 80–86.

Pentland, A., (2014), *Social physics. How good ideas spread – the lessons from a new science*, London, Penguin.

Perez, A. & I. del Bosque, (2013), "Measuring CSR image: three studies to develop and to validate a reliable measurement tool", *Journal of Business Ethics*, Vol. 118: 265–286.

Perez, R.C., (2009), "Effects of perceived identity based on corporate social responsibility: the role of consumer identification with the company", *Corporate Reputation Review*, Vol. 12 (2): 177–191.

DOI: 10.1057/9781137547378.0010

Pfaff, D.W., (2015), *The altruistic brain. How we are naturally good*, Oxford, Oxford University Press.

Pfitzer, M.; V. Bockstette & M. Stamp, (2013), "Innovating for shared value. Companies that deliver both social benefit and business value rely on five mutually reinforcing elements", *Harvard Business Review*, September: 100–107.

Phillips, R.A., (2003), *Stakeholder theory and organizational ethics*, San Fransisco, Berrett-Koehler Publishers.

Phillips, R.A.; R.E. Freeman & A.C. Wicks, (2003), "What stakeholder theory is not", *Business Ethics Quarterly*, Vol. 13: 479–502.

Pink, D.H., (2009), *Drive. The surprising truth about what motivates us*, New York, Penguin.

Ponzi, L.J.; C.J. Fombrun & N.A. Gardberg, (2011), "RepTrak Pulse: conceptualizing and validating a short-form measure of corporate reputation", *Corporate Reputation Review*, Vol. 14 (1): 15–35.

Popo, L. & D.J. Schepker, (2010), "Repairing public trust in organizations", *Corporate Reputation Review*, Vol. 13 (2): 124–141.

Porter, M.E. & Cl. van der Linde, (1998), "Green and competitive. Ending the stalemate", in M.E. Porter, *On Competition,* Boston, MA, Harvard Business Press, pp.351–375.

Porter, M.E. & M. Kramer, (2006), "Strategy and society: the link between competitive advantage and corporate social responsibility", *Harvard Business Review*, Boston, pp.78–93.

Porter, M.E. & M. Kramer, (2011), "Creating shared value", *Harvard Business Review*, January–February: 62–77.

Potman, P., (2011), "(Interview with) captain planet", *Harvard Business Review*, June: 112–118.

Putnam, R., (2000), *Bowling alone*, New York, Simon & Schuster.

Radjou, N. & J. Prabhu, (2015), *Frugal innovation. How to do more with less*, London, Profile Books-The Economist.

Rajan, R.G., (2011), *Fault lines. How hidden fractures still threaten the world economy*, New Jersey, Princeton University Press.

Rand, D.G.; A. Dreber; T. Ellingsen; D. Fudenberg & M.A. Nowak, (2009), "Positive interactions promote public cooperation", *Science*, Vol. 325: 1272–1275.

Rand, D.G.; J.D. Green & M.A. Nowak, (2012), "Spontaneous giving and calculated greed", *Nature*, September, Vol. 489: 427–430.

Reichheld, F., (2006a), "The microeconomics of customer relationships", *MIT Sloan Management Review*, Winter, Vol. 47 (2): 72–78.

DOI: 10.1057/9781137547378.0010

Reichheld, F., (2006b), *The ultimate question. Driving good profits and true growth*, Cambridge MA, Harvard Business School Press.

Reiman, J., (2013), *The story of purpose. The path of creating brighter brand, a greater company, and a lasting legacy*, New Jersey, John Wiley & Sons.

Rifkin, J., (2014), *The Zero Marginal Cost Society. The internet of things, the collaborative commons, and the eclipse of capitalism*, New York, Palgrave MacMillan.

Riolo, R.L.; M.D. Cohen & R. Axelrod, (2001), "Evolution of cooperation without reciprocity", *Nature*, Vol. 414: 441–443.

Rivoli. P. & S. Waddock, (2011a), "First they ignore you...: the time-context dynamic and corporate social responsibility", *California Management Review*, Winter, Vol. 53 (2): 87–104.

Rivoli. P. & S. Waddock, (2011b), "The grand misapprehension: a response to Aneel Karnani's 'Doing well by doing good' ", *California Management Review*, Winter, Vol. 53 (2): 112–116.

Roberts, P.W. & G.R. Dowling, (2002), "Corporate reputation and sustained superior financial performance", *Strategic Management Journal*, Vol. 23 (12): 1077–1093.

Rose, Jacob, (2007), "Corporate directors and social responsibility: ethics versus shareholder value", *Journal of Business Ethics*, Vol. 73: 319–331.

Rosenzweig, P., (2014), *Left brain, right stuff. How leaders make winning decisions*, London, Profile Books.

Roszkowska, P., (2010), "Reporting corporate social responsibility", *Economics & Business Administration Journal*, Vol. 2: 126–135.

Roubini, N., (2011), *Crisis economics. A crash course in the future of finance*, London, Penguin Books.

Ryan, R.M. & E.L. Deci, (2000), "Intrinsic and extrinsic motivations: classic definitions and new directions", *Contemporary Educational Psychology*, Vol. 25: 54–67, http://www.selfdeterminationtheory.org/SDT/documents/2000_RyanDeci_IntExtDefs.pdf.

Sacconi, L., (2006), "A social contract account for CSR as an extended model of corporate governance: rational bargaining and justification", *Journal of Business Ethics*, Vol. 68 (3): 259–281.

Sacconi, L., (2012), "Corporate social responsibility and corporate governance", EonomEtica: http://ssm.com/abstract=2102116

Schnietz, K.E. & M.J. Epstein, (2005), "Exploring the financial value of a reputation for corporate social responsibility during a crisis", *Corporate Reputation Review*, Vol. 7 (4): 327–345.

Schreiber, E.S., (2011), "A holistic approach to stakeholder relations to build reputation investment strategies", in A. Hiles, (Ed), *Reputation*

DOI: 10.1057/9781137547378.0010

management. Building and protecting your company's profile in a digital world, London, Bloomsbury, pp.69–80.

Schroth, H.A, (2011), "It's not about winning, it's about getting better", *California Management Review*, Summer, Vol. 53 (4): 134–153.

Schultz, M.; J. Mouritsen & G. Gabrielsen, (2001), "Sticky reputation: analyzing ranking system", *Corporate Reputation Review*, Vol. 4 (1): 24–41.

Schwaiger, M., (2004), "Components and parameters of corporate reputation – an empirical study", *Schmalenbach Business Review*, January, Vol. 56: 46–71.

Schwartz, B., (2011), "Practical wisdom and organizations", *Research in Organizational Behavior*, Vol. 31: 3–23.

Schwartz, B. & K. Sharpe, (2010), *Practical wisdom. The right way to do the right thing*, New York, Riverheads Book.

Sen, A. (2006), *Identity and violence. The illusion of destiny*, New York; London, W.W. Norton & Company.

Senge, P.; O. Scharmer; J. Jaworski & B.S. Flowers, (2004), *Presence. An exploration of profound change in people, organizations, and society*, New York; London, Currency Doubleday.

Sethi, S.P., (2008), "Globalization and corporate reputation", *Corporate Reputation Review*, Vol. 11 (2): 308–319.

Shiller, R.J., (2012), *Finance and the good society*, Oxford; Princeton, Princeton University Press.

Silver, N. (2012), *The signal and the noise. Why so many predictions fail, but some don't*, New York, Penguin Books.

Sinclair, A., (2007), *Leadership for the disillusioned. Moving beyond myths and heroes to leading that liberates*, Crows Nest, Allen & Unwin.

Sinek, Simon (2009), *Start with why. How great leaders inspire everyone to take action*, New York, Penguin-Portfolio.

Sinek, Simon (2013), *Leaders eat last. Why some teams pull together and others don't*, New York; London, Portfolio Penguin.

Sisodia, R.; J. Sheth & D. Wolfe, (2007), *Firms of endearment. How world-class companies profit from passion and purpose*, New Jersey, Wharton School Publishing.

Sison, Alejo J.G., (2008), *Corporate governance and ethics. An Aristotelian perspective*, Cheltenham UK, Edward Elgar.

Srivastva, S. (Ed), (1988), *Executive integrity. The search for high human values in organizational life,* San Francisco; London, Jossey-Bass Publishing.

Standifird S.S., (2006), "Using Guanxi to establish corporate reputation in China", *Corporate Reputation Review*, Vol. 9 (3): 171–178.

DOI: 10.1057/9781137547378.0010

Sternberg, R.J. (Ed), (1990), *Wisdom. Its nature, origins and development*, New York, Cambridge University Press.

Sternberg, R.J., (1998), "A balance theory of wisdom", *Review of General Psychology*, Vol. 2 (4): 347–365.

Sternberg, R.J., (2003), "WICS: a model of leadership in organizations", *Academy of Management Learning and Education*, Vol. 2 (4): 386–401.

Sternberg, R.J. & J. Jordan (Eds), (2005), *A handbook of wisdom. Psychological perspectives*, New York, Cambridge University Press.

Strebel, P. & S. Cantale, (2014), "Is your company addicted to value extraction", *MIT Sloan Management Review*, Summer: 94–97.

Sunstein, C.R. & R. Hastie, (2015), *Wiser. Getting beyond groupthink to make groups wiser*, Boston, Harvard Business Review Press.

Taft, J.G., (Ed), (2015), *A force for good. How enlightened finance can restore faith in capitalism*, New York, Palgrave Macmillan.

Taleb, N.N., (2004), *Fooled by randomness. The hidden role of chance in life and in the markets*, New York, Random House Trade Paperbacks.

Taleb, N.N., (2007), *The black swan. The impact of the highly improbable*, London, Allen Lane – Penguin.

Taleb, N.N., (2012), *The Antifragile*, London, Allen-Lane Penguin.

Thomson, S.; C. Rose & O. Risager (Eds), (2009), *Understanding the financial crisis: investment, risk and governance*, Copenhangen, SimCorp-StrategyLab.

Tinsley, C.H.; L. Dillon & P.M. Madsen, (2011), "How to avoid a catastrophe?", *Harvard Business Review*, April: 90–97.

Tucker, A., (2011), "Governance and reputation risk", in A. Hiles (Ed), *Reputation management. Building and protecting your company's profile in a digital world*, London, Bloomsbury, pp.11–22.

Tucker, L. & T.C. Melewar, (2005), "Corporate reputation and crisis management: the threat and manageability of anti-corporatism", *Corporate Reputation Review*, Vol. 7 (4): 377–387.

Useem, J., (2003), Fortune, April 14, 2003.

Vallaster, C.; A. Lindgreen & F. Maon, (2012), "Strategically leveraging corporate social responsibility", *California Management Review*, Spring, Vol. 54 (3): 34–60.

Verhezen, P., (2002), "A culture of gift exchanges", *Ethical Perspectives*, Leuven, September, 56–65.

Verhezen, P., (2003), "From a culture of gift exchange to a culture of exchanging gifts", *Jurnal Antropologi*, University of Indonesia (Jakarta), November, 101–115.

DOI: 10.1057/9781137547378.0010

Verhezen, P., (2008a), "The (ir)relevance of integrity in organizations", *Public Integrity*, Vol. 10 (2): 133–149.

Verhezen, P., (2008b), "The paradox of reputation", *Cultura Económica*, Mayo, Vol. 16 (71): 29–41.

Verhezen, P., (2008c), "Guanxi: networks or nepotism?", in Laszlo Zsolnai, (Ed), *Europe-Asia dialogue on business spirituality*, Antwerp; Apeldoorn, Garant, pp.89–106.

Verhezen, P., (2009), *Gifts, corruption and philanthropy. The ambiguity of gift practices in business,* Oxford; Bern, Peter Lang Publishing.

Verhezen, P, (2010), "Giving voice to a culture of silence: from a culture of compliance to a culture of integrity", *Journal of Business Ethics*, Vol. 96 (2): 187–206.

Verhezen, P., (2013a), "Do as the Romans do in Rome? A 'pragmatic' corporate governance perspective beyond ethical relativism in Asian emerging markets", in S. Rothlin & P. Haghirian (Eds) *Business ethics in Asia*, Heidelberg; New York; London, Springer, pp.91–107.

Verhezen, P., (2013b), "Managerial wisdom in corporate governance", in M. Thompson & D. Bevan (Eds), *Wisdom and complexity in organizations*, London, CEIBS & Palgrave.

Verhezen, P., (2015), "Fear and Regret – or Trust? From Transparency as a way to control to Radical Transparency to empower", an *International Finance Corporation (IFC) Governance Knowledge Publication*, Private Sector Opinion No 38, IFC-World Bank Group Website.

Verhezen, P. & P. Morse, (2009), "Consensus on Global Governance Principles?", *Journal of International Business Ethics*, March, Vol. 2 (1): 84–101.

Verhezen, P. & P. Morse, (2010), "Fear, regret and transparency. Corporate governance embracing disclosure and integrity", *WorldBank-NACC*, Thailand, Public Affairs Publishing, pp.27–54.

Vogel, D., (2005). "Is there a market for virtue? The business case for corporate social responsibility", *California Management Review*, Vol. 47 (4): 19–45.

Vollaster, Lindgreen, Moon, (2013), "Strategically leveraging CSR", *California Management Review*,Vol. 54 (3): 34–60. http://orca.cf.ac. uk/34595/1/Article%208o.pdf

Waddock, S., (2008), "Of mice and elephants", *California Management Review*, Vol. 51 (1): 103-108.

Walker, K., (2010), "A systematic review of the corporate reputation literature: definition, measurement, and theory", *Corporate Reputation Review*, Vol. 12 (4): 357–367.

DOI: 10.1057/9781137547378.0010

Walter, I., (2006), "Reputational risk and conflicts of interest in banking and finance: the evidence so far", Working Paper Stern Business School NY, downloaded: http://www.insead.edu/facultyresearch/research/doc.cfm?did=262

Wartick, S.L., (2002), "Measuring corporate reputation", *Business and Society*, Vol. 4 (4): 371–392.

Weeks, W., (2014), "Dimension 8: comparative position analysis in traditional, online, and social media channels", *A CUBIT-FOCuS Media Report*, Working Paper.

Weeks, W., (2015), *The Volkswagen case in Australia 2013–2015*, based on 2800 media reports, owned by CUBIT Media Research group, Melbourne.

Williams, R.J.; M.E. Schnake & W. Fredenberger, (2005), "The impact of corporate strategy on a firm's reputation", *Corporate Reputation Review*, Vol. 8 (3): 187–197.

Wilson, D.S., (2015), *Does altruism exist? Culture, genes and the welfare of others*, New Haven, Yale University Press & Templeton Press.

Wilson, D.S. & E.O. Wilson, (2007), "Rethinking the theoretical foundation of sociobiology", *Quarterly Review of Biology*, Vol. 82: 327–348.

Young, S.B., (2015), "A better social contract for financial intermediaries", in J.G. Taft, *A force for good*, New York, Palgrave Macmillan, pp.19–31.

Younger, R. & G. Giambona, (2011), "Framing reputation: vague concept or measurable business asset?", in Hiles, A. (Ed), *Reputation management. Building and protecting your company's profile in a digital world*, London, Bloomsbury, pp.33–44.

Zabala, I.; G. Panadero; L.M. Gallardo; C.M. Amate; M. Sanchez-Galindo; I. Tena & I. Villalba, (2005), "Corporate reputation in professional services firms: reputation management based on intellectual capital management", *Corporate Reputation Review*, Vol. 8 (1): 59–71.

Zingales, L., (2008), *Oversight Hearing on Causes and Effects of the Lehman Brothers Bankruptcy*: http://www.ilsole24ore.com/fc?cmd=document&file=/art/SoleOnLine4/Finanza%20e%20Mercati/2008/10/intervento-zingales.pdf?uuid=880e2f34-9465-11dd-8554-b299b4e00502

Zyglidopoullos, S.C. & D. Mchardy Reid, (2006), "Managing corporate reputation within the Chinese context: future research directions", *Corporate Reputation Review*, Vol. 9 (3): 155–161.

DOI: 10.1057/9781137547378.0010

Index

DOI: 10.1057/9781137547378.0011

DOI: 10.1057/9781137547378.0011

DOI: 10.1057/9781137547378.0011

CPSIA information can be obtained at www.ICGtesting.com
Printed in the USA
LVOW07*0105121215

466384LV00006B/74/P